Hopelessly Romantic Poems Collection

Hopelessly Romantic Poems Collection

By

Rhonda Jennifer Dolen

ParisBurg Publishing
2011

Copyright © 2010-2011 by Rhonda J. Dolen
All rights reserved

2011 Edition

Artwork on front cover:
John William Waterhouse, *Boreas* (1903)
[Wikimedia Commons]

ParisBurg Publishing
www.parisburg.com
www.parisburgpublishing.com

ISBN: 978-1-877981-17-3
(Trade Paper)

Dedication

Dedicated to my family and friends.

Most of these poems were written from 1999-2008.

I am steps away. I can see it. It is the most devastating, most confounding, most real realness, it is living, it is light beams, it is the end of nothingness, the end of hum-drum, it is a different life, it is dripping from our beating hearts into the world, to disarm it and link it to our dreams.

A note to the reader:
These poems are not categorized. A romantic does not categorize hopelessly romantic poems into little boxes.

Contents

Bands of War: 7
Index of Poems. 153
About the Author. 157

Bands of War:

I watch you and I wonder now
If you can but know how
My heart beats and my hands
Tremble, fingering our wedding bands
I sit beside you while this war still goes on
I am awake far before dawn
It was one second, dear
And you were almost gone
One second separated from all the rest
In that sad, miserable place of hate-filled contest
I never knew such a bond
Please respond
All I feel is well past beyond
What I ever knew existed, and it still here lingers
As I clasp your fingers tight
And pray you will make it through this night

Silent Pianos:

Oh, not again, again
It seems I never can win
If you could stand outside, looking in, at a window in the rain
If you could feel this pain
If you knew what it's like to have everything locked up
And give nothing from your over-running cup
If you woke up every day a fine-tuned piano silent, dusted
A fine show piece wondering if you're rusted
A cold hand, un-warmed, blood running through
A silent, unvoiced masterpiece no one knew
And if Grace Kelly missed her cue
And if tomorrow was overdue
Would little flowers remember words never spoken?
Would the world be bereft, with a memory token?

If men all wore blindfolds all day
And were deaf and mute
Until I was old and grey
Would there be a trace
Of grains down an hourglass chute?
Of smoldering ashes never burnt?
Of dead words I never learnt?
If songs were always sung where no one could hear
Would it get me through another year?
Is it a shame or is it something honored
When dusted, safe on a high shelf is the vase instead?
In it, flowers dead
Beside it, books unread
Soft things, unsaid
A mind fled
Tell me it's no great concern
To live life to yearn
To give every tear and fear, raise your voice loud and clear
And in the end be still austere
On shelves we put the things we honor
The things we prefer
What is simple and easily understood is kept near
Away from what is mere
Silver, mere gold
And we grow old
With cracked pots and dishes
That sit near and watch us fulfill our wishes
God help the silent piano, dusted flute
The crystal vase un-chipped, up high
The wax fruit
And I

The Matter of Things:

In love with love
If you'da asked me to straight up marry you
Baby, it woulda been you and me right on cue
But then I would have done that before
With one of the others I did adore
And I'd do it with someone else today
So, what can I say?
I'm in love with love, dear
And I'm still standing here
Waiting for my lover love to get swept off its feet
By me and my mad dashin' passion
So, light my fire
Ever higher
Love I'm chasin'
That's what I'm facin'
Lace and rings
And dishes and things
Are all there waitin'
All I need is someone over who is worth statin'
Vows to
A friend true
Passionate kisses
Makes me his Mrs.
I love so rarely, sparked in the first instant met
It's a rare man who on me can cast a spell
They're usually too easy to forget
And I hardly ever want to know a man well
But when fire meets fire beware
Keep me away
Or like blissful moths we fly two passionate spirits drawn to the glare
A dangerous flare
Like a sweetly answered prayer
Our love will be like rebels against the nothingness
And when and with who is anyone's guess

But beware the woman's eyes
Too wise, they catch you like diadems and surmise
If you have what it takes
And are made of what, despite all her mistakes, that for which she aches
If you have that fire inside
And from the world you have been sorely tried
If you have eyes wiser than years
And can understand there is more than appears
She will see you
And all this she will construe
It's long overdue
And if you by chance pursue
She will meet you halfway and with eager love true
But understanding is rare and
Beware you think you do
In love with love
You must find a love potion numbered down to
Chemical magic
DNA tragic
Hit the chemistry books
Pop the hood and take a look
Love is found rare
And that's the matter
There

You Are Realness:

That little gesture caught my eye
Baby, let it out, let it fly
It's true, you could learn a thing or two about charming
But, I find your innocence totally disarming
I know you're really not very handsome
But your looks turn me on, hold me ransom
And the things you tell me are so silly and serious
But they make my knees jelly and my heart beat delirious
It's true you're kind of goofy and no romancer
But you turn me on like some kind of expert enchanter
Can't you see my dimples dancing across my face every time you're near?
They're coming out 'cause you're here
And you're so strong
And I can't see you treating a woman wrong
If you could read my dreams
What would you do? Because I'm afraid, it seems,
Something's got to give sometime
And I'm afraid of being wrong, stopped on a dime
I'm wanting you to see
You could be with me
I'm scared you're just being nice
And it's some roll of the dice
But you could
If only you would
There's no reason you shouldn't
No reason you wouldn't
If I could ever read eyes
If I could communicate with sighs
Would promises, you, make?
What kind of steps have I gotta take?
I want an answer; so, I've got to use that tact
Make my interest that known fact
With some indirect obvious phrase
There are so many ways

I'll know right away if it was worth my daydreaming
And scheming
I have to take that chance
That you'll catch on and want romance
You're free
I just need to know where you want to be
So here goes
Do you want me? Who knows?

Like Religion:

Love is like religion
Adherents find sin
Claim apostasy
Live in epiphany
For it, so many kingdoms fall
In homes, castles to us all
It has its cherubs and its covenants
Cherry-cheeked children and vows to break
And perchance
You wish to make
Little promises, say little prayers, display ceremonial flare
There are no shortages of opportunities
To learn the rituals to say you care
Whether it has meaning, too, none of us know
But some of us think so
It sparks wars and has its own casualties
And who knows if its call to battle is just a patriotic tease
Of patriotism to false gods and defunct symbolism
Or if it is eternity's ever-shining ethereal prism

Risk Inverted:

Are you both characters in that play?
Tell me, but I do what I may
I can't deny what you say
I've got a new affinity
A deeply set priority
Left that past
Look at it, fast!
A moving effusion
Ancients called it poison
And who says it's not chosen?
A fever with the shakes
That takes
Button it up then
Take it down, pay it down
Patch up the sin
Wiser win
Leave it set
Pick up your bet
And walk away from the table
Cut the car's cable
Look out, here comes stable
When wrong threatens to whisk
Is wisdom risk?
Is it too unfamiliar to step out, away?
To give it up - today?
Can safe be fun?
Which way is the one where I run?
And from what is it from?
What's the end result, the sum?
Risk inverted
Men converted

Fireflies:

Brilliant little lights
One by one shine
In the soft, summer twilights
Heralds of a fairy world divine
Old legends of them talk
Being amongst them
It's like through the stars we walk
Each one shimmering like an instant gem
How many worlds I can see at night
When I sit and watch them
Each one a sprite
In beautiful flight
Shimmering through the enveloping night
Of fireflies, in this winter firelight,
I sit and dream and write

Unrequited Questions:

Well
Why the hell
Don't you want me?
I can't see
Why you're so blank
For whom do I, that, thank?
I've got this crazy side
It's true, I confide
Gotta go a little fast
Gotta outrun it all, make life last
I'm quite composed
Not quite what was supposed
I hear a sweet song somewhere
I hear people gathered who care
I see happiness floating in this world of ice
Every day is a throw of the dice
For us all

And I'm in life for the long or the short haul
I wonder
Every time I hear the shocking sound of rain and thunder
Where am I now
Whispers of too many worlds.
How?

Send Heaven:

Sweet and funny
He's so sunny
What is behind that look
Does he know what it took?
To not smile at him today
To pretend to miss him in the fray?
I haven't allowed myself to care
I am afraid of being there
Will he ask me?
Can he really be?
Are his eyes dancing my way?
Is there a real love up for play?
Can you un-break my mind today?
Can you not make me pay?
It's kind of light
But that just could be right
I'm so lonely I could die
Please don't make me cry
Please say something
Happy tomorrows bring
I saw you looking at me
Could it be?
We might be great
And you might be first rate
I just can't take any step towards you
None at all, it's true
Not after the years I've been through
Not after the blue

You crossed my mind
But I'm in a bind
I won't even approach you at all
That's an obstacle not small
I'm stuck in a protective shell
Please stop the hell
While I was lost
Were you counting the cost?
Are you thinking of asking today?
Heaven, won't you send someone right my way?

Dreams Hanging in the Air:

I think I found a dream today
In the midst of the fray
Your eyes were looking my way
And all I can do is pray
You seem so safe, like a real place
Nothing complicated about your face
It's what we make of it
I can't on all my hopes sit
I wonder if you'd stay in sorrow
And really want to be in my tomorrow
I wonder if I can have that place my own
A new home
All ours and all how we shape it
At night the lamplight circle of ours lit
A dream we both share
A commitment to care
And defying the cold world we dare
To make our own little world fair
With rules and hope to spare
The fabric of our hearts try never to tear
We are nothing but our promises floating in the air
Amidst the horrible burdens that we come to bear
But we have a little dream floating in the air
A place in our minds to catch our breath, to share

Our love is home and a new start in this cold life here
A pledge to, though far, always be near
To the dream that is happiness and love
To the hope that always aims above

Devastated:

I'm completely devastated
It's a little belated
I just kind of go
You don't have to know
I don't know how I set so many fires
In so many hearts, misguided desires
I don't want them
I'm not supposed to need a him
It's a little strange
I'm a little deranged
I have really great problems and fears
I have really lucky tears
I've got nothing to make me cry
And I'm not supposed to have to lie
I really don't understand
I am not supposed to need to hold a hand
I haven't cried in years
I haven't got time for tears
Did you notice
The pain inside this gorgeous, weeping, moonlit Lotus?

See Me There:

See me there
In a world I know not where
Fires burn
From love and faith we turn
Our days are numbered well
In years or a day we fell
We're all in the past
And there will come a last
I see a fire burning in the distance
I feel it when on creaking floorboards I dance
I hear it in the notes of music floating
When with my children I am doting
I see a dream, a fire, kindled wishes
More than ethereal kisses
Somewhere past or present, there or then
I know there is that thing, very real
And I don't know why or when
But I know I can feel
And I know it was and is and reverberates still
Twilight or dawn, I wait until
All masks are lost
And paid are all costs
Long after it is missing or never found
I will still, to hoping, be bound
For it is all the mystic fire living
All the point of us giving
It burns in my hands, like the heat off my skin
Tell me we all can win
I am one light, one fire
Lost in this hideous, dark, cold mire
I see more than I will tell
And I know more than is well
To know
Or than I can show
A darkness threatens hope tonight

Don't let it snuff out my little light
They come and prey on my soul
Those thoughts that take their toll
Leave me alone cruelty and cold
Leave me before I am old
Where is the time when I am away?
What is the price I still yet pay?
Don't leave me nothing now
Don't leave me asking how
I worship at the altar
My faith does many times falter
I fear for tomorrow and the next
With what is left of this wreck
Steer me clear
Away from fear
Bring me away
Don't ask me more toll to pay
You say we don't labor in vain
And life is more than pain
I still see your frenzied fire burning
And all of my heart for God is yearning

Spirits:

I won't wait anymore
Today, I saw a look that changed my mind
A second that stands out in time
The thing is even if "the one" isn't you
I know for today, that second, you could somewhere love me too
In spite of your better judgment
In a quirk of chemistry that missed the hint
I know I don't have to wait long
Even if him, and him, and you, are gone
I felt my power standing there
And I know that in another world you could care
In one second I will meet him or it might be
Even you

I can finally see
I'm amazing too
My heart dances; it's been broken so, so much
And in a few hours, a few weeks will be that one's touch
If he loved me, I would love him more
And if you love me, we'd be in love forever, no - much more
And if the other man I saw today loves me someday
I will love him in another way
But I'll love him as well
Because though I rarely love - yes it's hell -
I know I may love that man
Yes, I can
So, walk away if you dare
Keep it so you can't care
But someday when you're waiting in line
Waiting to buy a paper, you'll think of some quality of mine
And see my face and think of smiles
Though we will have traveled 10,000 miles
And so will he, and so will he, and so will he, and he as well
And that lump in your throat, you'll be able to quell
But, I will be happy too
I haven't yet stepped out to my cue
But when I do
Roll out the red carpet of my heart
And take my part so well
Never will there be a happier dream
And never a more well-mended seam
At least that's what we say
On that day
When we truly love
The gift of spirits and anchors from above
And I wait, well into my life, for the eyes
That to me direct their sighs
For the most amazing magic on earth is real
And I will feel it, I will
And I carry that magic until
All the world finally stands still

Wants:

I want you
I want the moon
Freeze this moment
Freeze this now
Take your eyes away from there
And put them on me
Again
Take my hand; you are my friend
You stand with your back against all the wind
That's so cold outside
My thoughts, I don't bother to hide
Nor you, tonight
And I can't believe
We almost didn't do this
This so right
I miss your hands in my hair
Your lips there, there and there
What wouldn't you give
To have a little fun while you live
Everyday, every way
You're just the sweetest irony
In my world right now
And how did it turn out so real
So, suddenly right
I gather up little flowers in my thoughts all day
And you little whispers of what you feel
And then we get away, get to be
With each other, un-stutteringly free
You could make my hands shake if you want to
I could make you, blinking in disbelief,
Just standing, feel a sudden rush
Of all the good things
Who needs to be around kings and yachts and diamonds and to
Travel miles
All the while there's love like this
What is this not

It's everything
I dangle my thoughts before you when I want to
About later
And you dangle your words and your eyes tease
What can't you say to please
I'm so glad we didn't let
This walk away
And what a gorgeous day
To wake up next to you
And hear you say
What a gorgeous day it is when the sun hits my hair
While you're laying there
Well, this is sweet

Even, Even If It's Just A Fling:

I won't ever move my lips to tell
Too many times I fell
All the years I've watched others find a space
And then I looked at my pretty face
But discovered others are more full of grace
And I got put back in my place
When you have really, really bad luck
Continued optimism turns things amuck
Just give up and close your eyes
And realize there's not going to be a prize
And time suddenly is just like a joke
And if you could cry the tears might choke
You in your restless sleep
But you still think your love of life will keep
Though it throws at you oceans and rivers too deep
You refuse to not swim
Though it throws rocks up too high
You refuse to see a precipice too steep
Because you have everything
And life has been too good
Every day is such a flowery, beautiful spring

Why then is all you ever want
Crazy, crazy love
Even, even if it's just a fling
And why do you have to keep looking above
To ask why you aren't satisfied with everything besides
And not know why there's an ache that never subsides
The only way to be happy is to ignore
To frost the world before
It gets to you
So you just give and live
And hope some day
You can learn to forgive
Your lot in life
Or else to outlive
All that's ironic
All this life iconic
And find the one thing you always looked for
Before
Until you decided to just ignore
And to embrace the dance floor
Live to explore
Give it a go always once more
Never keep score
Endlessly adore
See the beach shore
The ocean floor
Do what's been done before
And what is more

Oxygen:

Save me like fire
Save me like rain
Never again to disdain
A-light with desire
Billowing clouds float by
In a perfect, dangerous sky
Cocooned in a diamond-studded waste-land
A ball spinning through, not spun by any hand
Liquid water, oxygen, flame
All so very crawled-together, so very tame
I whisper still
Come what may, come what will
Hallelujah, hallelujah
From the wild dream woven air

For Lying Eyes:

If I could have that night back
I would gladly part life at dawn
For one fleeting touch of your lips I want, wanting me
I would lie to myself that I would trade eternity
For that conversation sifting, settling on the air
For that one second there
When we stood eye to eye
For that night, I perpetually, somewhere inside, cry
If I could have made it longer
Shown my affection stronger
If I could have stolen some kisses
Fantasize you, tangling lips to lips, wanting me even one second
Your Mrs.
If laughter could have been a little more
If I had refused to leave that night so early out that door
If I had played your cards back
Would I, my emotion, still lack?

If I could have only, just one love-filled kiss
And left not one thing else amiss
Would I still be dead inside
Even if your eyes only lied?
If I could be ignorantly full of bliss
For one moment, one kiss
Would I trade all my life I know today
And all tomorrows gamble away
Chancing that is all I need yet to truly live
All I ever asked anyone to give?
Yes, I would
If ... only I could
It's such a small request
Such a poor trade for settling in to other-worldly rest
But I can't have that night back at all
And I walk the earth like a ghost
I can't listen for your call
I can't even imagine what I want most
I can't make other choices
And somewhere an angel rejoices
As I miss out on false kisses and pain
What would I give to have a broken heart, all that could remain
But I have instead an ice-cold freeze
Lips no longer able to form the word please
A swirling dark
A frozen, cut dead spark
All my passion, incoherent and full of dreams
Lost chances gone when that pleasant evening passed
With reams of mildly interested talk
I can't remember when I was ever in love last
All I want is a lie
For wanting to be hoodwinked I cry
Not even a kiss, not even a loving hand on mine
I'll carry my unbroken heart, chipped ice until the end of time
I can't even look up anymore
Rather than live like a tomb
I'd rather be even his whore
But I can't be that at all

I'm frozen as good as the sweet bird's call
A song bottled and sent in for packing
And the world goes on, only I lacking

On Heaven or Earth:

We fell
Like some sweet drunken spell
Now I wish you well
I miss you my friend
And if you tend
To what we have
I'll see you here
Or there
And one time again
You and I will spend
The riches of time then
And there
Or now
And here
I wait to see if you return
My heart has come to the time
To burn
For our sweet rhyme
I yearn
And whether on heaven or earth
I will touch you again
I will ... all my faith
For what it's worth

That Look:

What the hell did you just do?
Looking at me
Your eyes on fire
That can't be true
I'm happy free
And you're another liar
Get away
You're not going to make me pay
I'm not gonna be stuck under this sunshine ray
I've left before
I know there's more
I've left before
Let me show you the door
Don't kiss me
I want you to miss me

Misdirected Wrong:

I'm not cutting you any slack
I don't want you back
You had my heart on a silver platter
Tossed it to the floor, heard it clatter
You're what was the matter
A heart-hitting batter
I think ice runs through your veins
A good heart he feigns
The devil never looked so good
And I never thought he could
You're one investment that depreciates
It's only fate
You're like a lost foul ball
You cut my engine, made it stall
I have no use for assembly-line pain
The feeling didn't continue to wax and wane

It disintegrated like so much lit cotton
Poof it's gone
As fast forgotten
For what it's worth, it was strong
Just misdirected and wrong
On a shadow that didn't exist
And then you let me have your fist

Not Bored:

I'm not bored
It's been fifty and four
And you love me even more
And I feel you with every step on every floor
Wrapped around me
Like a halo, or something more
Teach me why I found this
Tell me why I die every time we kiss
Teach me why I found this
When everyone else seems to miss

Spark and Crackle:

Kiss me crazy baby
I didn't say maybe
It's all fun
I'm not particularly sure
You're the one
But I like the allure
I like to laugh
And I'm not gonna do any math
Or maybe you?
You say you're so true
You notice me nonstop
And your eyes never shop
Can you always make me spark and crackle?

With my expression on fire
When you promise that flag football tackle?
When I'm eighty and three
Will you do anything for me?
Is my mind where it's at?
Or is it not that?
Or you, yah you,
Tell me why you smile at me like you do
It's all play
Until I decide to stay
I want something I can't walk away from yet
Someone who isn't placing a bet
'Cause I was more fun than starting to run
And all he wanted was to get
His feet wet
Let me know we just met
Fire up my intellect
But only if his effect on me
Makes me not want to be free
And how rare is that
Without it, love goes splat
Hell, if it ain't any fun
I'll turn around and run
It's all been done before
I want more
I never wanna know what's in store
I want to forget how to keep score
I want true fun
Pedal to the floor
Forevermore

Nothing Less:

Jam it
Slam it
Make it fit
Dress it up with wit
Form it and fashion it
Pretend it's passion
I'm tired of dressing up days
And dreaming of love so many ways
I don't want to spend my mind
With someone whom I'd never find
To light a room with fire
Like I would light his heart with desire
I won't settle for less
I'm getting out of this mess
No more settling for one moment of being bored and annoyed
And being accused of having toyed
With you or you or you
I want to love you too
And I don't; so I walked
And they talked
I want it all
And I won't settle for a small
Serving of grace, fire, ice, passion
Emotions smashing
Into one another
A real lover
I want something better than okay
I want love, friendship, fire - every darn day
I want peace and calm and sweet
And so until we meet
My heart will alone beat
I won't miss you
In another life perhaps?
You'll find me too
Grab my hands in complete happiness

We need no maps
You won't catch me settling for less
You won't catch me unable to profess
Unwilling to confess
And I wouldn't settle for less
Here's to unreal desire
Unconfused fire
Of which two minds never tire
Who each other inspire
To champagne chiming
To perfect timing
Here's to wanting the most
Having the courage to let ghosts
Fall away
And find the one who will stay
And know exactly what to say
And want you more every single day
In that incomparable way
And that is the only dream to which I tonight toast
Here's to carpe diem crazy
Here's to dropping dreams till they're hazy
Here's to sense, never tense
Here's to what I'll confess
And to nothing less
Nothing less
Not ever
And here's a toast to tamed, unchained, fired, inspired forever

Love is a Comedy:

Blind me
Bind and entwine me
With daisy daydreams
And floating fields
And rip up the seams
And wield
Cotton-candied whispers
And tell me you love me till I'm sure
Make it fun
So, this time
I won't run
Our hearts together tease like a rhyme
Baby, with you it's sunny
And when you say you love me, it's just funny
And then you throw a pillow at my face
And I fall
Oops, did I lose my place in the book about how there's no more
And how we're all just so poor
Because the covers just hit me in my face
Well, if that's the case
Here's a pillow back at you
I told you I could do it too
This really can't last
Because being in love with you is a blast
You love me inside out and over and above
You claim it's the first time you're deeply in love
Take that feather pillow slap
I can read you like a map
But I was never very good at direction
What rhymes with direction?

Sparked:

I gave you my heart, I did
And you can't take away what you said
And what you made me say
Shut the door tight on all those days
Your greatest irony
You thought you walked away free
But my face now is on every corner
And you never, ever loved her
Nothing to show you, you said
I would have raised you on that
Instead
You can't get me back
Sweet words and kisses
Oh, your near misses
Rumors and lies?
Whatever; I'll trust them first
Over your disguise
Trusting you was worse
Kisses, candy melting whispers
Sitting by the fire understanding her
Sweet scented cares
You hadn't, apparently, the nerve to dare
And I know your heart for me beat
You, I refuse to ever again meet
Mock me again
Taunt me too, one more time
But your sin
Will never scar my soul
Go ahead and lie

But know you threw my heart away
And when you have occasion to,
On a faraway day,
Remember the ember of everything
I sparked in you
Rue, baby, rue
Because you did it to me
Broke me, can't you see

Sitting With God:

Don't unbreak my heart
Don't make this a new start
Don't kiss my hands
Don't want to hold my heart with gold promising bands
Don't kiss my mouth with hunger and with life
Don't ever ache to make me a fiery, unbridled wife
Don't kiss my needing, giving, secret soul
Make sure this world takes a toll
Don't kiss my breasts awash with worshipping thought
Don't to a higher power throw your lot
Don't do a damn thing without a disastrous fight
Don't part the curtains on the first night
Leave me now
I don't want to learn how
To love anyone
In all this world there is no one, there is none
I want to sit and cry with God for empty men
Every thought of their's against finer things is a sin

It Burns:

It burns
It turns and turns
Five thousand hours she yearns
For one second she learns
It's a lesson
It's a blessin'
It's my new way
It's that new day
Sweet new friend
The beginning at the end
Cherish me the most, like a diamond, dear
With your perfect timin', I never fear
I just need to rest my head
After what was said
But can't you just stay?
Oh, we have found a way
Never say not to try
Never want to make me cry
Learn from these tedious hours
Your mystical powers
From here and there
To wherever - where?

VHS Control:

Leave her
Why would you spend her life and yours
Trying to deceive her
And yourself that you're in love, and really hers
Just so a little sooner you have kids to kiss
And have someone you're obligated to miss
When she's at the grocery store
But you don't; oh the horror
Or better yet
Marry her like you almost did before
And wake up screaming, caught in a patched up net
Wanting more
It is fine
But therein will be the prison you give your mind
Finding you've mistaken worshipfulness for a good friend
And something richer you purposefully rend
It and offend it and turn it cold
Dare it to go away, grow old
It's easy to see unclear at that distance
Don't mistake a hand of aces for a chance
You can't take
Something unnerving and fake
She is just kind company; she is nice
But she's without fiery passion's spice
Passion is not an automatic death sentence to "kind"
To think otherwise is to forever your life rewind
But you can only play what you did
And can never change the channel to a different path
Go ahead and pretend it's Pandora's box and shut the lid
But life is inching away; you do the math

What's Me?:

Am I too right
To be here tonight?
Am I too pretty for this place?
Do you see eyes too wise in my face?
Am I too pristine for that route?
Am I too real for you to try to tout?
Would it be too much of a chore?
Or am I really just a detestable bore
And not quite so lovely?
I don't know; I can't tell what's me

Leaning Against the Wall:

I used to sit on the stairs
And lend my shoulder to the wall
Trying to forget my cares
Sitting as close to you as I could, trying not to bawl
But you weren't there
I might even step out into the cold night air
I wanted to run to you and cry
But I knew that wasn't my
Place
And no hands held my tear-stained face
And yet I was happy there
Finding dreams floating around, in with the lace curtains and cold night air
It was really strange, don't you think?
And when I think about the wrongs, my heart sinks
I would sit and hold your hand and dazzle until the sun could rise
I would, but there was no way, I realize
And somewhere thoughts went up like beautiful things, floating
And there was a dream, and sometimes I caught myself hoping
But let's not stray too far toward happiness
And forget everything real, this boring mess

I just could never believe
And I think I always need to leave
Because I know you'd hurt me
I'm not very interesting, I see
To some I am so exciting and right
But I refuse to wrong myself with the wrong man and the wrong night
I only want my own dreams
And I won't pretend to be their's, to sew up their seams
So, if it's a poor dream, fine
But, it's still mine

To Be Mended:

I love you
It's quite unfortunate
That's true
Wilting, dead roses rest
In a forgotten bouquet from the best
Night in both our lives till now
It's impossible to forget how
It felt eye to eye
I think of it and cry
I bury my face in the skirts of my hanging wedding dress
My entire life is a mess
Won't you stop, won't you seek control?
You are taking my dreams, a heavy toll
Stop courting death, my love
I look at you doing these things, and I can only turn above
Why are you asking me to live like this?
What will I do without my favorite kiss?
Why are you lying to me?
Why are you refusing to see?
Don't you love me,
The one whose heart washes over your soul like the sea?
What couple ever made a sweeter dream?
Come back and sew us up at the seam

While the rip can yet mend
Because now there is someone who on both of us will depend
I didn't want to tell you with my face covered in unhappy tears
But I am falling victim to all of your fears
Make it right, be a man
Without you I can
But I don't want to
There is no one who loves me like you
You're the only one sincere
The other side of the mirror
Come here and take both my hands
With me, finger our bands
Commit back again to me
You are a best friend, maybe the best is yet to be
Don't not try
Don't make our vows a lie
Clutch my waist and hold me in the middle of the swirl, the rain
We will make each other more sane
Sitting on the floor together tight
I would be happy if you would sit and talk with me tonight
All it takes is your heart really fighting for me
Again and I'll see
A way back to better
There has to be
Your dreams build the way, letter by letter
Take back your heart first
The rest will work its way well, not become worse

Christmas Morning:

Something like Christmas morning
A magic that doesn't fail me
With you I am besotted
An intensity allotted
By the gods in a depth-filled sky
And I transcend the question why
In your arms, attended to by angels
Rise above all the headaches and tangles
Best of friends
To my heart tends
Never lost
Never thrown about and tossed
Before me the enticement of your eyes is dangled
And a song named love is jangled

Feelin' Belief:

I can feel it just underneath
Beyond belief
It's just out of reach
And a thousand tomorrows couldn't teach
Me more than this feeling
From which I'm reeling

His Choice:

That's it here
I have no more to give
My heart like twisted roses jaded
There will always be more fear
I hoped my heart with yours to live
But I must confess I awoke to all my dreams faded
My confessions fall on deaf ears
For so many years
I mean it now
Don't dare to ask me how
I think I feel nothing more
When my heart mildly beating you held before
Don't throw your pearls to swine
This a Bible verse I feel written on me letter upon letter
Dreams sometimes unwittingly fetter
You stand in your corner fearless
I'm sorry, you didn't register it was a near miss
But a miss still
Tell me will
Your heart jump at the sound of my voice?
Will your spirit rejoice
At the glimpse of my face?
Will you step off the curb in haste
And rush to touch my hand?
Forgetting you've taken your last stand?
There on a repeating CD track
Your memory will forever take you back
I have no more patience for entreaties to conjure up spirits
Did you hear my heart leave, did you hear it?
You took your future with both hands and buried it
And your candle will never again be lit
A last call rises from the dead bar's dust
And you must do what you must
Stare at your untouched glass
And make a choice
Now or let it pass

Used Too:

I really don't need you
As I stand here, thinking it through
I don't need to not need anyone either though
Wouldn't you know
That every pick is wrong
And the cards fall at the end of the song
I can't hide in the dark forever
I thought I'd do this never
But I decided if it doesn't matter to you
It doesn't matter to me
And I can be like that too
You'll see
But I hear they like us all better jaded
Our dreams forever faded
If they like us at all
Oh, it's the last call
You know what that means
And I used to have dreams

Bar Sense:

You're there
What do I care
Insipid gestures don't compare
To that across a crowded bar stare
Time is spendin'
Tell me where I've been
I've got happiness to spare
And frequently I mean to care
Take a piece of happiness from me
When I give it away, I always got more
I've got it right, I'm set for life, see?
I'm not looking for some distant shore
It's perfection just as it is today
And I ain't got no more to say

I Got S'More:

Diamonds are loaded up around me
I choose not to see
I have money
Okay, that's right, honey
But, I got something to wake up for
When I look at your eyes
I just want s'more
We sit together under big open bright skies
You are so wild and right
And I could sit here all day and all night
And just listen to you
And I guess you wanna hear me talk too
So, baby get the car out and let's go
'Cause we're gonna ride away from this crazy show
I like that you surprise me
I don't see like the other girls see
And that's why you just don't wanna be free
So, hey
Make my day

Rue:

Give men a beauty or a whore
And they will love the whore forevermore
Though the only difference between the two
Is one is free to love and one is for sale to you
They chase the empty and the dead
Afraid of having someone better in the bed
They have no sense in choosing friends
And tantalizing, angelic, exciting women they rend
There is no way to tell them they are lost, every one
And none of them differs, none
The curse of woman was to so need men
But they don't need us, and it's a sin
A woman is nothing without an admirer
Only a self-consuming fire
Our lights go out too soon in this empty sphere
And there is never one near
When you need one
And they're never fun
Never were creatures more selfish and empty
I want the day none of them tempt me
Little children without direction or
Perception
Our curse
Was far the worse
For now we work sunup to sundown too
And I know our entire lives were meant to rue

I Can Hear It:

I had such bright dreams once upon a time
But now I'm around you again
My spirit falls silent like a mime
Oh, the presence of you makes me into a sin
I want to hurt your feelings for what you've put me through
I want to actually do
Something that will really throw you off
Because at all my accomplishments you just scoff
And all my good behavior makes you grind me under your heel
Even more, while you try to make it impossible for me to feel
You say I can't ever find anyone to love me
You said I was a loser even when being crowned with honors for
The world to see
You anger at any movement that you deign upsets you
No matter how innocent and lacking in meaning, you can still
Turn the screw
To you I'm a whore
Even though there was never something I more
Wasn't and to you I'm rebellious, hateful and unable to learn
To the rest of the world an eager, sweet woman of no concern
To you I make plots and always have the worst intention
To anyone sane, I'm the essence of innocent convention
I wish to defy your perception in every way
I want to be so loved, so successful that I prove you wrong this Very
day
I want to fight against the picture of me you put in my spirit
I can hear my soul fight against it, I can hear it

Electric Air:

You were like a freedom to break the spell
A moment that was all mine in a tricky hell
I could pretend that there was somewhere good here
And I could to sweet dreams walk precariously near
There is a danger in the world but what of it?
There is always something more or less to get
And we are always upset by this
But sometimes you can find in a kiss
Something sweeter than you'd dare to admit
Something to which you're not sure it would be fair to commit
There are tragedies lining the roads of our every mornings
Very real, frightening, serious warnings
Moments are counted like the grains of sand
And sometimes you just can't reach out a hand
The air rests against us, electric charges through us sent
There is no way not to breathe and there is no easy way to circumvent
But embrace the gifts we get here in our cages
As our mysterious dreams filter down through the dead ages
Hail to the mysteries of life, of lives
In a second what is life-changing sometimes arrives
Step carefully through the distracting maze
And maybe you will find new ways, more clearly gaze

Awed:

I have an as yet silent destiny
Which nothing can ever take from me
It steals from me any thought of ambition
For there is nothing which will delay that transition
To its heavy burden I am in no place to but affect submission
The future haunts me, a daunting apparition
The world like a gilded clockwork turns and turns
And all my thoughts like ever-present stars full of formidable power burn
And I wait in a quiet intermission
A strange and unlooked for position
On the heels of buried tradition
Things wilder than those among which move the magician or the politician
I prepare feeling somewhat resigned
By all of mankind confined
It is a hard thing to move in masked circles that later flit across a stage
A tired world, a looked for age
For every word, one day will I carefully have to pay
And maybe that's why I pretend it isn't that way
You cannot run easily on moving trains
Or deny what's written, even if it pains
Everything like a giant crescendo
Tempered innuendo
But I don't think ignorance is bliss
And so I hesitantly pretend to accept this
I flee from success
Because too much of everything I possess
It tempts me not to try
It makes it suitable to lie
Some people find power of that sort not to be resisted
But I quietly observe, confident, still not yet to be assisted
Moving in the air tonight is something and I ponder the still, large sky

The difficulty of wanting to defy, but being helpless to deny
I wait for an unlooked for moment here
And what was boring, of no consequence becomes sought after there
I made a choice not to guard myself much
But it is difficult to feel such
Things here and know that it swirls yet closer
Like a strange symphony, by a well-known composer
I am a little awed, the magnitude I can barely comprehend
I did not ask for it, but it will descend
Take this away from me
But it is only in vanity I successfully flee

Fairytales:

Cinderella, Vanity Fair,
Pride & Prejudice
The stories are all there
Fabled fairies and Rapunzel you know
Grace Kelly, Audrey and Monroe
Too many pretty faces
Stories leaving traces
And what will they say of you?
You've got a story too
You sparkle like that tinsel on the tree
You didn't captivate them there
But you captivate me
So many stories; who can care?
But what about this one here?
The real and the fake ones still on this sphere
Being told over and over again
Weaving tales, the storytellers spin

Cross:

This is it, today
I need out
No more of this, no way
You always scream, always shout
Your words are the cruelest I have ever heard before
There's always more
I remember being hit
Over what? It didn't matter, did it?
The words are as ugly as can be
I never know what will aim them at me
I live in fear
Right here
I don't talk about it, and I never will
It just seems to put the chill
On everyone's good time
And it never crossed the ultimate line
Besides, I haven't got the money to leave
But someday, freedom I'll achieve
I'm counting the days 'til I'm out of my prison
Finally driven
Away with lifted chin
Still okay within
When it's good, it's good
And when it's bad, it's really bad
Do you think this, you could have withstood?
And yes, sometimes, I let it make me really sad
They'd all be shocked
If they knew how I'd been knocked
With words and threats and fear
Control, that's what he wants, dear
I never know what will set him off or where
And that's the heart of it there
I remember words that killed me inside
If you could only know how I had cried
Yes, my life is perfect

Just what you'd expect
Except, the abuse
It's really no use
I did it all because I had to
But it was never enough
Are you looking anew?
And yes, I know what it's like to be tough
I just usually ignore it now
I'm astonished I learned how
But I could tell you stories to make you wonder
Amazed, I never went under
I reacted by doing so well
I thought if I'd just excel
Be everybody's belle
I could break the spell
But it's really not that bad at all
I try to think of it as a small
Cross to bear
I try to care
Besides I chose it now
I knew this was how
It would be
But I needed financial security
God help me find a man
Who honors me
And can
Help me really happy be
It's really a small cross to bear
And I chose it, and I know life isn't fair

Waiting in Crystals:

Trillions of crystals
Cascading down from the air
Each one an immeasurable work of art intricate, rare
Falling softly into icing
From the heavens up there
A craftsmanship, a sculpted wonder enticing
A blanket the color of angels' wings
This makes me think on many things
Rare and special, valued and dear
As I stare out the lace draped window here
Even in a shower of crystals of ice
We don't know where to turn for advice
Your wonders entice me to look towards paradise each day
I didn't think I would go this way
I'm waiting on a call
From someone who makes crystals from this sky fall
Hold my hand
You understand
Watching such wonders planned
I'll go at His command
I always thought you'd stand by me
And tonight in crystal rain
I finally see
The purpose, the plan
I don't know where or why this wonder began
So much more complex than a crystal melting away
Just as fragile
You don't know what to say
Here in the chill
But you will
I lift my eyes up to pray
Not this day
Wait longer to take me away
Still
By the window sill

Crazie:

You're kissin' me
I'm thinkin'
That's how it's done
Don't you think so, hon?
When you start winkin'
I can see you drivin' me
Crazy tonight
Found, tucked-in just right
I neeeeeeed you darlin' love
You're Mr.-Sent-From-Above
Come on let's get lost in passion
Unexpected, lost that fear of crashin'

Games:

I don't like your games
I don't wanna play
I don't need to read off names
When I asked you to stay
You burned me through
Makes me rue
The day I met you
I don't think you noticed I'm not going insane here
I haven't got another tear
Not one
I'm done
So, keep losing me more
Just like before
I refuse to keep score
I'm not your freakin' encore
Don't play with fire baby, listen
Or you'll get burned
I'm not planning on throwing my life away for your kissin'
I've learned

I don't play golf, football, baseball, or heart-break
You got what you wanted to take
If you wanted more
You never would have kept score
I'm ignoring the plays, dissin' the field, and the fight-song
Baby you just keep getting me wrong
I would only listen to hear you say you gave up the play
I'm not especially enticed by the fray
My heart is out, a life is dedicating to me - wow
I finished grade school games, I'm with the big kids now
If you want to be with them
Compete with him
You gotta play it straight
But it's half past too late
And my friends don't play games either
And I have neither
Patience nor the will to suffer
Over an unsure lover
Or a friend who can't be bothered to be in my world tonight
In being nothing . . . I have no delight
Scores of dreams knock at my door
And I am waiting for
Nothing
Leave your boxes of games . . . always a game
For me games will never appear the same

Wake Up Love:

Am I on another constant rebound?
From what and how?
Is this real?
Is the frost melting; can I really feel?
Have I crossed that point, met that man here?
Or will I wake up too late in a year?
Is it the spell of lonely tossing, crying, aching?
And finding now peace, for love, it mistaking?
Or did I wake up to what I never knew I wanted before?

And found a new world promising, unsure what's in store
Through an open and inviting door?
Surely, there are many more?
But why am I drawn back to this quiet place
And the sweetest soul I see in your face?
Why do I want nothing more than anonymity with you?
Why do I feel like I've never felt so true?
Why do I see you as a dashing king with a halo on top?
Why do I never want your kisses to stop?
Can it all be so simple? Can I really be so happy today?
Was I feeding myself lies, lost in a fray?
I never knew I wanted this
All I ever think about now is your enticing kiss
I want that life with you, away there
I want you to wake up and play your fingers through my hair
I want you to hold my hand through it all
I want to hear you answer my voice when I call
I want you to admire me like that everyday
Like I want you in every single way
I want the unexpected, but how can I want so much so fast?
How do I find such joy in such contrast?
You hold me like a precious crown
You sweep me off my feet out on the town
By just being so sweet
The kindest nicest guy, you're so complete
I can see it
I want you, I admit
Why are you shyly asking how?
Can't you see how much I want you now?

Untiring:

I have been so hurt many times before
I can't be hurt anymore
Not so much, not by a man
Don't think you can
The last time is always the worst time
But now no more lasts, only firsts sublime
I grow tired easier, weary faster
Of men who think to be my master
When will they learn
It's not again to be my turn
I won't accept one minute of one thoughtless, cruel
Men who insist on playing a fool
Love is not for play
And offering nothing will never entice me to stay
The good fight is beautiful today
In this messy disarray
And I will fight it well
And fall under no chaining spell
Only spells that hold scintillating life, peace inspiring
Will hold me forever, with me never tiring

Animated, Not to Be Blamed:

It's really kind of calm
An infinite psalm
I sit and read by the fire
And you'd never know I ever touched desire
I am rational and cautious too
Led by rules and times and hues
But you'd never know how I like to bend the rules
Men, you're all such wicked fools
You see me with my perfect life set in stone
A placid, peaceful kind of tone
But under it, rapid in my veins

Is all of spirits, dreams, heaven that in human blood remains
We move about to routine
And forget the magic of each scene
I am like that recorder, that sets down history
Giving color to make it reading rich, full of mystery
I do it with everyday
I am always at play
My imagination like a wild thing untamed
So alive, something for which I can't be blamed
It is passion
With me, it's never out of fashion
I'd make every moment like a game
But one with rules, one sweet and sane
Time is flipping the pages just right
And I am waiting on the chair with my thimble tonight
I sit so quiet
But wouldn't you know, if I choose to share
There's an enviable riot of richness
And animated motion there

Words:

My world is made of words of magic, of power
And hovering beneath them, this very hour
Is a carpe diem kind of fire
The kind I know you stutteringly admire
My beauty can be touched you know
It's not always just for show
Your kisses I hunted with whispers on the air
While I was sitting there
One question and words could have tumbled out
To make you in shock look about
And wonder how the world turned so rowdy and right
And where have you ever been before this night
My words still tumble out to lovers in my dreams
My heart is busting at the seams
I would give near all my life

To be my love's only, to be a besotted lover's wife
I would jump on a plane tomorrow
From mysteries and dreams to snatch and borrow
I would tease the tempest's everyday boredom and sorrow
And dare you to really live and risk this with me
Can't you see
I've never had the chance
I never with someone I loved dance
I have words bundled up inside
I am wild, crazy, and I'd take you on this ride
I am sunny, safe and saved
Into heaven you'd be waived
I am bait and tackle too
I am everything, everyone you ever wanted to love you
My mind is like a precious, jaded pearl
A flower waiting to unfurl
If you ever kissed like I would you kiss
There is nothing in life you have missed
I am what you should trade the world to find
It is my mind
If you have my affection dear
You should risk every danger, embarrassment and fear
To hold my beautiful body near
I was put here but for a brief hour
I have spent it like I was locked in a tomb with a one-way mirror, a moonlight flower
I can but dream of a way out, and you refuse to see in
I am waiting for the wall to tumble
For my loneliness has made me desperate, far too lost and humble
But you know my words are made of breath floating on powered air
Tell me, could the wicked Fates of us care?
I am beating on the door with both fists
I know so much that is right exists
My words tumble out like boxed fairies set free
What carpe diem kind of man wouldn't want with me to be
This day, this hour
This way

You Don't:

We both know you don't
Love me
And you won't
My heart, spirit see
I think I cracked when your words like knives
Threw my fantasy world and sent us into separate lives
I think you never loved anyone
I think I was never the one
I think promises die on heartless cold lips
And the lifeline, it slips
I thought you would scramble back for the jewel
Of my heart, but you were only cruel
And I see I am forced to admit I'm a fool
My heart like silver-lined stars, turned to water, sparkling, racing
A salt water I cannot drink, a drowning I'm still facing
I see precious things are not so valued
A world mad, a heart cold, I conclude
"Love me!" screams the scented perfume of my soul
Be careful what you extol!

Seas and Deserts Part Us:

Dear, please come here
Be near
Speak words of comfort, Sweet
Let us not talk of things concrete
Tomorrow will part our worlds for time indefinite
We have no choice but to submit
But I will wait for you
And you will look for me too
When you come back home to me
And you and I can finally just together be
Seas and deserts will part us
But I must profess
They will never make me love you less

Until we speak again, hand to hand
I will wear this band
I love you
And that is the help I give, all I can offer to do
Until I see you again
I can only dream of when

Bare Floors:

You had my heart like a silver tea set on a platter
To the ground you tossed it to crash and clatter
I gave you numbered dreams
And you ripped out my seams
Sell your life, your soul
That will never make you again whole
How can you stand losing me
When you're left with the rest, left dead and free?
You see the crows marching one by one
You know you were awed and undone
My words melted you like sticky cotton candy
And wasn't your availability handy?
You wanted me right
For me you would damn near even fight
You let it slip from your hands dear
When you didn't reach over and kiss me
You lost to fear
When you could have seen in my lack of fears where you'd be …
Lost and gained and sainted and tainted
Take the measure of your losses
And come crawling back, battling the end as it tosses
You back to the sharks that eat at your dreams
For me they wrote love songs in reams
Which you would to me play
All the lovely day
You made me your goddess
And I made you my little brass-plated idol
Desperate, you know no other woman will convict you so

Don't you know you never wanted me to go?
Tearing at the cloths of the lost
You, wept, tried at the cost
One hand out and you would have found
Something wild and sound
There's lace under the drawer
In the case
And what's more
You leave in haste
Remember how good words taste
I will remember what my dreams are for
Now
Miss me dearest, miss the kisses planted on the air
And the passionate embraces you missed by
Just one neglected stare
On the bare-wood floor
While the worlds in our ears roared
But you let me pass by
Tempted me to cry
Catch me one last moment here
You never once held me for a frosted second near
I'm only here, only fear

This Off-Course Bird:

I write everything from my heart, red, beating, dark, wide
It's a place to start, a place to hide
Tomorrow I will put my mask on bright
Everything is just so right
And I never cried, not once, not there
I haven't ever had a care
I haven't got any secrets, not ever
I am so lost, even though clever
I make myself another face
I wrap my world up in lovely lace
I wear heels
To disguise the spills
I color bright
To fight off night
Like a bird off-course, alone
I flutter, falter to all nowhere I've flown
Can't the world see there is really something I need?
And can they once not expect me to uselessly proceed?
Or do the Fates just smile knowingly
While glowingly
I pave my road to hell
By where all my dreams fell?
Do I look a little too bright, glitter a little too much
Yet shrink from the slightest touch?
Is all the world in on the lies
While this off-course bird still falter flies?

This Broken Light:

I'm sitting here screaming right now
Asking how
I see my life, all of it empty and wrong
And I hear song
Draining out of my soul here
I am less, I live in fear
But I fear nothing anymore
Nothing that's ever in store
Because what would I miss if I was taken from this place?
No, anything and this I could face
All I want is a home safe, sweet and bright
Away from this eternal night
I want to have a place to go
To know I am clasped to someone real
I want for once, love, to know
I want for once, peace, to feel
I want to hold my heart in my hands
And be lifted off of shifting sands
I wish the world could change for me like magic today
There has got to be a way
I wish that I had a home I had ever really known
Un-chisel me from stone
Light a fire around my heart's icy case
Tonight this moment, this place
My dreams hang like broken fragments in the uninterested air
Tell me there was ever someone who would for one past instant care
Make my home tonight
Help me this broken lamp to light

The Dark:

First of all nobody knows
And nobody cares
I don't know where the pain goes
And the world moves unawares
In the dark, in the light
I sought a way out of my night
Did you ever get hit?
Shaken?
Was life for you ever something mistaken?
And yet here I sit
Strange it doesn't matter
Even when it happens, my world falling in a clatter
Like pots and pans and no one took a stand
And I never had a hand
Holding mine
And maybe I never will
And maybe that's fine
I can keep going until
I won't
Don't
Did you ever hear words so wrong
You didn't think you could ever be strong?
Did you ever cry until you were lying broken
Sick, everything unspoken?
Did you ever get used to the chill?
Did you ever wonder if you would ever feel?
Did you ever hate men?
Did you ever think you would never ever win?
Did you ever over achieve
As a way to deceive?
Did you ever weep and die inside
Just wanting to get off the ride?
Did no one ever perceive
The depth of how you'd grieve?
Did you ever need to move away
And you didn't have the money

And have to stay
Hiding in what's sunny?
Did you ever run screaming outside
Without shoes
And then you learned it was better if you lied?
After all, this isn't news
Did you ever need someone, anyone so much?
Just one moment's peaceful touch?
Did you ever fall so hard you couldn't fall anymore
And learned that everyone would adore
You if you just smiled and laughed and did
Even if the furthest parts of your soul were in a skid?
Did you ever not have a home anywhere?
Did you ever sit and stare at your bare
Wrists and wish that it was over now
And wonder how
You could ever wish that when you're really so
Very happy and you know
You won't?
But please don't
Did you ever have nothing to complain about at all
Except everything in those walls?
Did you ever have to agree and make nice to save
Your sanity and yourself and did you ever behave
Just to get to where you could be you?
And did you ever wish there was someone true
To lean your shoulder on and be safe with now?
And did you wonder how
You ever got by every day without what you need
And with nothing on which to feed?
Did you ever love your friends and your life and your blessings
That you'd never go confessing?
Did you ever lie to yourself every day
So you would stay?
Did you ever say it's not as bad as it used to be?
Did you ever long to be free?
She just wants to be loved now
She just doesn't know how

Down on Your Knees:

Is that you?
Down on your knees?
You mean you really felt it too?
And your vocabulary found the word please?
It's me you loved and need?
And you concede
On me you trampled and sought to mislead?
And my heart you only wish to heed?
And you only want all my hurt to recede?
And my love is your second creed?
And off of hope you wanna feed?
Your heart you want me to read?
And you're ready with your life to proceed?
You say you just wanted me to know
Before I go?
And you're begging me to see
That you really love me?
Are those the questions I have to answer now?
I'm scared and I don't know how
Do you know how to not break a vow?
Do you, everything I need, want to allow?
I stand here on a line
Tightrope walking this time
Should I cross?
What is the potential loss?
My decision is up in the air
It would be so easy if I didn't care

This Exquisite Need:

This exquisite need
To its sirens I did heed
I have given all I can give
And so I go back to live
More than before
Once cracked
Such a door
Never closes; that's a fact
Asking again, yet again did not receive
That doesn't mean this feeling's gonna leave
It gets transferred, deferred
By it, I all over get lured
I'm in love with love always and forever
Even now still a pleasant endeavor
So, my hunting arrow fell again
Hey, someday I'm gonna win
Is fiery emotion this strong a sin?
Cause if it is I've long past given in
My heart is crazy, yes it has been
Only hastily, lightly controlled from within
You can't extinguish these spirits in my eyes
God help the man who tries

Live Like Light:

I am afraid of death
And it stirs me to life, suddenly living
Your words move me like the flower, Baby's Breath
Caresses the air
Their fairy-like beauty, seduces my hard heart to giving
Clasp my hand and every moment against death to dare
I want all my life with you to share
But if not I won't complain it wasn't fair
Because there is no promise I'll know when I've said my last prayer

Even if there was no you
I want every moment to live believing it's true
For the promise of you
And for the promise of a divine Creator
And of Heaven above men's hearts
I'll follow and lead too
What other many wishes could be greater
Than these few
On Earth I want to play many parts
And they try to chart the stars
But I don't want to be charted for you to easily construe
Oh let me play wild
And never love mild
And send me dreams big and loud
But don't let me be proud
We'll all fight the good fight
And hope we're right
Live every moment until it's your last
Like it's your last, unreasonable fear to surpass
What is the point
If you don't
Let go the un-sensible fear
So draw near
To God and His fire alive
Finally, not waiting for light to arrive
But lighting your candle, your lamp light
In this dark night
Sit on the table
Don't let them put you under the counter if you are able
Be that lamp light circle bright
Fight to see with heavenly sight
Love like one of the good few
Until life bids you adieu
Be sweet and gentle, kind and try
For you never know when you have to say goodbye

Treasured Now:

I can't help but stare
It's like I haven't got a care
This is it, enough, I dare
You are so there
Finally a peace on the air
A person with whom I can share
You won't, like paper, my heart tear
And shifting sands I don't have to bear
So mystical the magic sprinkled air floating
My life with happiness this feeling is coating
I'm sitting without fear
So very near
My hands are shaking now
And I am not afraid to ask how
When did heaven touch my hand?
Where did I find someone who wants to stand
By me?
My heart wants out of the prison of being free
Oh chain me up, kept safe, boxed, wrapped like treasured gold
And keep me loved and guarded till past even when I'm old

Throw Away:

Throw it away
Take that gorgeous Da Vinci or Van Gogh
Ya know?
And just trash it
Take the dart and hit it right in the eye
Take a stained glass treasure
Worth its measure
In gold and call it old and break it into pieces that splinter
And into a dead world enter
Don't take pretty things and smash them
Don't forget to kiss him!

Don't hang up on philosophers and don't draw your drapes on a sunny day
To make it go away
Don't cuddle spiders and rats
And don't let the wind have your favorite hat
That's
The first rule of living
So, when you're mad, forget it, and practice giving
Or you'll smash that Van Gogh
You know?

Hey, Listen:

So, I'm a little surprised that I love you
But I'm a little crazy
As anyone can view
A little sassy, but I find it a little hard to face me
And all the energy I have sometimes hides out, goes low
Because I think of all the places I can't go
But, when you're captivating me
It's kinda easy to see
Everything's totally carefree
'Specially when you're kissing me!
So, let's sit by the pool
You'll
Fall off the edge into my world, jump into the water
Hey, runnin' around with me, it's the cure
For a beat-us-down world, topsy-turvy
And my road is just a little bit curvy
Some say it's the straight and narrow
But, I can't stay on it when life hits me with its arrow
So, if you wanna fall in love be aware
There's a certain matchless fire, a certain dare
In my lips
Kinda like the sips of that there drink in your hand
A throw back bourbon with just a little bitta kick
A little bite

So, please don't fight
You can still sit on that comfortable bar stool and drift
And dream, and your thoughts to heaven will lift
I'll whisper those words about all those great ideas and dreams
And naturally expect to get back reams and reams
Let's go for metaphors and rhymes
Careful it's fragile that whiskey glass
Remember that when you're making a pass
In the bar or on the field, however many times
Did you ever just lay down by the ocean and hear the waves
And wish you weren't surrounded by a world of knaves?
Did you ever wonder if sugar and spice and everything nice
Is sometimes all just an empty glass of salt and ice?
I swear I've got that tequila somewhere
To take away all your cares
Would you take away mine?
Put up a welcome sign?
There's a beautiful tomorrow with peace and roses and spice
Oh, wouldn't some peace, love and understanding be nice?
Call the wild hearts from our humdrum souls and spirits
Hear my heart, hear it!
Bets and games and cowards run me down and my hands shake
Everyone is so fake
Come and sit here and whisper of tomorrow
Of a world near
Somewhere where people don't fear
Rip out my emotion someone, tame it
I've given up
Maybe someone should shame it
It must be unwelcome like salt and dust
And maybe I should take my energy and spirit and paint it with rust
I want to run with giants and with men
I don't want to hear that being happy and kind is a sin
I want some attention and someone to listen
I guess that's what I'm still missing

Ocean Shore:

That was a little bit rash
But, hey you were like my Johnny Cash
Let's just not talk about it now
How in the world, how?
I've got my fingers crossed it's not
It's a little late to see such a lot
But really, what should he expect
Why live so circumspect?
Why always do everything right?
Why never be wrong, not even one night?
There's a little bit of ocean hitting the shore somewhere
There
And wildflowers growing in fields somewhere
And sometimes there are days without a care
I'm not sure this ship is ever going to land
And frankly I don't care; I've taken a stand
This probably won't get me anywhere
And I, frankly, wish I didn't care
And there is a big blue ocean under the sky
And I just can't wait to say, "Hi"
To the lovely days ahead
There, it's said

Mi Amor:

Will you light up my room?
Will you do it soon?
Will you be more than a mystery?
Can you see
How to touch my heart today?
Do you hear it beating off the charts now?
And can you feel how
I catch my breath when your eyes meet
Mine and do you sense how I barely can feel the floor beneath my feet?
How is it you attracted my attention?
And what would I do if you were to mention
That you like me so?
And don't you know?
I find you breathtaking
So many times I've been mistaken
But you seem so utterly sweet
So disarmingly off-beat
Touch my hand today
And I'd not be able to find a word to say
I see everything good when I look at your eyes
I can't believe you would ever tell lies
I see someone completely nice
And I am so ready to throw the dice
Haven't you been taking steps towards me?
Oh wouldn't that be heavenly?
I can't help but dream
Did you notice how I beam
When you pay attention to me?
Oh can't you see
How you delight me with your kind words to me?
How I would love it if you could really be
That someone?
I'd feel so safe and happy and wouldn't you adore
Me and be such a sweet friend, mi amor?

Mi, amor - wouldn't that be nice, so right?
Oh, that's what I'm thinking of tonight
Tonight

Other Vision:

Too long suffering in silence here
In a place of unmitigated fear
Put down your hand
Leave your hateful stand
Let go my life
Take away your knife
Leave her alone
Are you utterly stone?
I live in a cage
Surrounded by rage
Go away
Wish you wouldn't stay
You are the voice that keeps me from sleep
You are the jailer who does the keys keep
I live in a gilded prison
Give me someone with other vision

It's the End Now:

The candles are chimeras tonight
And I think I've lost this fight
They light up your face before me
Though my eyes can clearly see
Your love has died
And then your hand from mine shied
How is it you have found another?
So much more of a lover?
And your contentment is your holy grail
And my real love must fail
To mean anything to you at this point
My destiny is out of joint
My hands cleave to something gone
And I will have to wake up to a strange, unfamiliar dawn
And I will just have to get used to missing
Our wild, love-filled kissing
Because you have moved on ahead
And we'll go home to our empty bed
Until you pack your bags and finally close the door
One last time, forevermore
Maybe tonight we can forget
Hold each other and ignore it

It's Your Call:

Hey baby
Haven't heard from you lately
You're so sweet
Why the retreat?
You're all sunny
And so funny
Take a chance
Steal some romance
From life's shackled days
I could love you always
But it's just a haze
You're so fazed
I'm bored with datin'
Sick of waitin'
It's your call
Like always, you'll stall
Well, life's candles are meltin'
My eyes are tiltin'
Up there
To dreams a-floatin' away
Love's nowhere
You could say
I could care
Up for a dare?

Et Tu:

Don't you know?
I love you
So go
Et tu, and you?
Feeble faith of mine
God, feed me a line
Eyes staring without blinking
Cold shoulders without thinking
Find me a map in this dark, caved world, this place
What else, what else . . . must I face?

Love Dances:

Love Dances
On heaps of broken chances
It is fire and ice
And it should never employ device
It is there
Even when the rest of the world doesn't care
It can rise from the dead like the Phoenix in history
A beautiful mistress of time, full of glory
It lurks in every soul
It is life's eternal goal
It is more than many things we think it is over time
It is the soul and it is the rhyme
It is the lover of life in us all
Without it our hearts break and stall
There is no way to forget its power
And it is there every hour
It changes form like magic waves
It can knock us out, blind us like the worst haze
But it is ever present over the sphere
Form-changing, vanquisher of fear
Once awakened it lives in ashes

Sometimes, hope, it brutally smashes
It mixes, matches, dances, catches, lifts, inspires
It is a symphony of heavenly fires
It is a dream
A tired scheme
But it is all there ever was and will be
It is the essence of all that is me
And you
It is you too
It is the one constant that stirs against evil and hate
And to lose it is one of the very worst fates
Keep it alive, lift your spirit to wide, expansive heaven
And relish in all you have been given
Dare and dream and fight to keep love
It is the sweetest, dearest, real-est gift from above

Lit:

I will no longer accept this bitter cup of pain
And my living is not in vain
Rusted for lack of touch
I want what is over-much
Gone is that tired reserve
Up with verve
I want what I want
And I don't even need to hunt
It's everywhere
In every stare
Find me a place away from the glare
I swear I will care
My demons still stalk
But that doesn't mean I can't from them walk
I will find it
The whole world is lit

I Have an Obligation:

I waited for you to tell me something
Anything
But all I felt was the sting
I wanted to hear from you
I wanted to know what to do
But day after day
And night after night
You never found the way
To my door or tried it right
And I realized it was I who was delusional
As usual
I couldn't wait for kisses
After all the near misses
I wanted everything now
I wanted to know how
I waited for some indication
I was wracked with temptation
I had that desperation to feel some sensation
Was that look an aberration?
Was there no real relation?
Was that not animation?
Was it never admiration?
All I could clearly see was frustration
And I realized I was just insane
And I failed to see what was plain
You couldn't have been moved by me
And I lacked the ability to see
What was obviously real
Because all I did was feel
And I left and gave away my kisses
To someone who proclaims how much, me, he misses
Every time I leave the room
Whose passion for me threatens to consume
My doubts
Because about me he is so devout
He became my constant friend

Everything good he did intend
I was lifted to a sweet place
In his embrace I emanated grace
I never thought you thought of me
Or that we could ever be
Then someone said speak now or forever hold your peace
And we swore never to cease
I didn't regret
But later, by chance, we met
I saw a look on your face
My memory will never erase
If that was the case
Why did you not, after me, chase?
Why did you let him love me uncontested?
You never requested
Now at night sometimes I am restless
And my perfect world is a mess
Now I have to confess
From him there are thoughts I now suppress
And sometimes a shadow crosses the path
As I sit here forced to do the math
You gave me no reason to wait
And then you were far too late
I gave myself away
And today
I am in utter disarray
Would someone tell me how this could happen to me?
That I now dream of being free
So that my skin tingles with the thought of a distant foundation?
A determining conversation
A lost elation
A missed destination
A creeping desperation
A distant hesitation
A killed motivation
An unfortunate fascination
A reawakened inspiration
Unwelcome information

A sick dedication
A sad transformation
A new isolation
A remembered expectation
As I watch my new generation
I am filled with revelation
About my situation
There can be no communication
Of my painful, new animation
I have an obligation

When We Are Old:

When you wake up a broken man
And all your dreams have passed you by
When your head is gray
I caution you not to think back to today
When your pockets are still empty
In your last days, don't remember me
When you see that I have everything you meant to have someday
Do not on your lips, my name say
When I have shown myself to be more than you ever imagined
Do not to me, your regrets send
When you sit alone in the dark and pick up a magazine
In which I am, do not say you couldn't have seen
When I am rich and well-fed, skinny and protected
Don't say you wouldn't have suspected
When my words make men burn with fire
Don't pretend you never had desire
When I prove myself blessed more than you ever thought
Don't imagine what you could have sought
When my dreams are a startling reality
Don't come and weep before me
When you don't try
Don't expect that my heart holds left one tie
Don't expect to be other than a stranger walking in cold
For those old times, they will be old

And so will we
You never had the gift to foresee

Pointless:

I've heard sometimes things crack
And that they can never be got back
That sometimes people lose meaning
All possibility of on anyone leaning
Sometimes while living one can be still dead
And the looks on one's face can then never accurately be read
Sometimes, one thing is too much
Sometimes there is too much weight in a touch
Sometimes one can lose all sense of care
All knowledge one is even there
And one puts on a mask
And no one would know to ask
Life becomes utterly boring and completely dull
And then you are capable of a miracle
You can do great deeds
Because you have no needs
Because your faith is dead
And you are too well read
What is pointless is cruel
And what isn't pointless makes one a fool
Betrayal is a cold cheek to turn
A hard lesson to learn
A dark night
A stop-all-the-fight
A take and not give
A hard thing through which to live
To give to nothing
Is really something
To see empty air
When you thought something good was there
To become blank
Who is there to thank?

No Tatters:

Is there a name
For this kind of pain?
Make it stop now
Please, show me how
Come on, tell me I'll wake up fine
And nothing's ever on the line
Tell me it's always okay
Even though there's no way
Tell me I don't need anything
And put a band-aid on the sting
Tell me there's always someone better
And to my dreams I'm not a debtor
Fuel me up on nothing at all
Tell me the dictionary lacks the word enthrall
Buy some flowers
Let's pass away the hours
I'll shove the memory in the trash
Or in my secret stash
No one will know
And they say this is how we grow
Nothing matters
And no one is ever in tatters

But I Just Don't Want It To:

Of you I dream
For you, in my heart, I scream
My days lack wonder now
I forgot how
My day is jam-packed dull
Of thoughts of you, there is never a lull
What cruel things come from Fate
What happened of late?
Why do I think on you?
Why does it affect me through and through?
It will someday leave I know
But I just don't want it to go

Seeing in the Dark:

Deepest love
That fell from above
I could sit at your feet
And of your words eat
You are the sweetest thing on Earth
I highly estimate your worth
I adore your eyes
They make the proverbial sun rise
I dreamed of you when I stared at the night sky
I heard you in my heart when I asked why
I saw you in my sleep
My love was wholly deep
You filled me with wonder and verve
I was hoping you just didn't have the nerve
You were like a diamond that wasn't polished much
And I thought awhile on how I wanted your touch
I felt thrilled by your voice
You were my number one choice
I was besotted with you

My admiration was true
I saw a brilliant creature
Not a special effects full length feature
I saw a man who was kind
Tell me was I entirely blind?

One Soul Lost:

Screw you boy
I'm not some toy
You're icy
Your dreams are dicey
I'm like Aphrodite wrapped in silk
You're always fixin' to bilk
You use
You light my fuse
You take love and trash it
My heart, you did bash it
You're a sociopath
You sit there and laugh
You think you can treat people like somethin'
You stepped in, just like nothin'
People throw themselves at you, you ham
I did even though I know you're a sham
I desired you in spite of your callous ice
The way you don't even realize you use device
I thought you were a king
But are you really just a whore
Using women like a fun fling store?
You're like a self-destructive drain
And into my sunny heart insist on bringing rain
I thought you were wise and wild and sweet
Kissin' you would have been a treat
For you I'd have walked at least one mile
I would have been impressed if you tried to beguile
I overlooked the way you wouldn't treat me like anything but dirt
And left me constantly up in arms hurt

Some day the women will see you're standing over a pool
Thinkin' you're cool
Starin' at your own reflection, in love so deep
While they will always bitterness reap
But it's so fun to be treated like that when it's you
Because you're so smart, handsome and dear
Who cares if you don't love your lovers true
But someday they'll notice, it will be clear
But it will be okay with them still
Because you're handsome, smart, sweet and a thrill
But that's just cheap
It's not deep
He could have been a king they said one day
If he'd realized, changed his way
But he was knee-deep in quicksand
He never even reached out a hand
He woke up one day and felt empty and cold
And terribly, terribly old
He cried his heart out every night
And wondered why he didn't do what was right
His heart was broken for all time, for every sunrise
He was not wise
What might have been
The saddest words in the English language he will speak
Then
And he cries what you sow you reap
He will want that time back, but it will be too late
Tell me was his path the work of fate?

In the Blink of an Eye:

In the blink of an eye
I found I was missin'
Sweet unbelievable kissin'
I met the star
That takes me far
I danced the dance
I fell in the trance
I met the king who takes me there
What a way to care
We used words to wow
And time saw how
I was tired of fightin'
Quick, just like lightnin'
All those who hurt me
Who did desert me
Will they look at you and wonder
How you could steal their thunder?
Because you say you will
In your arms I thrill
Never lie to me
I don't want to see
Tears on my face
Please, just erase
All those who walked by
And all the times I asked why
Sweet dreamer man
Tell me to put on their faces a ban
And keep makin' me laugh like that
Oh baby you're up to bat

Somewhere Out There:

Somewhere out there
Don't know where
Is one with the right stare
Who is always fair
Who has eternity for me
Who can teach me to see
More
And who is still in store
I have time to look
I have a world to be shook
Words are the liquor of existence
From whence
He will announce his presence to me
And answer a forgotten plea
Even if I forget I'm looking later on
When I find him
I'll be inexplicably drawn
And the feeling of confusion's disarray will dim

Already Given:

I already have my love
I found him in the deserts' wind
And rain clouds and rainbows above
I found him in the palm tree fronds that send
My mind to thoughts of the ocean brushing my feet
And my heart will never rend
It's so sweet
I know him like the backs of my hands
And I already held his hand on tropical sands
We talked for hours
And I feel him still when I walk through fields of flowers
He loves me
Even though he's gone away to see

The face of God in paradise
So his memory will have to suffice
I already found him in the water's glimmer
And I know his memory will never grow dimmer
I already met him on the cliffs' edge
And we already made our pledge
I will sit with you and talk today
But know this
I've already given my heart away

Faust:

Spritzed ice, rum, coke and cherries
Palm pilot, blackberries
Porsche, BMW, Mercedes
Out on the town with my ladies
Searchin' for some Mr. Rights
Laughin' as we start some fights
Calls keep comin' in now
We don't know how
We'll keep their names straight
Out again too late
Where's the rose, where's the prince?
Who takes hints?
Where's the fire, where's the flame?
Where's the one who lends his name?
Got my strawberry margarita frozen, salted
For ladies in distress nobody's halted
Court-side seats to the joust
We're all just another name for Faust

Do This:

Sunny days
Funny ways
Hold my hand
Come and stand
By me
Got that key
Got that lock
Pay no mind to the clock
Buy me flowers
Talk to me for hours
Tell me everything now
Show me how
Be nice
Take leave of device
Walk me home tonight
Make it right
Open my door
Love me more
Help me carry that
Walk over my welcome mat
Feed me chocolate kisses
Make me your Mrs.
Bring me this
Retrieve a kiss
Don't take my bad mood
Come with me when I shop for food
Admire my silhouette
Make me your favorite bet
Shut me up when I'm mad
Make it better when it's bad
Together we'll hit the town
Can't even find my frown
Admire my sexy dress
Make me 'fess
Kiss me crazy dear
Never let me fear

Accept my caresses
Be maddingly attracted to my tresses
Let me tell you how you're so hot
Make me appreciate what I got
Like my smile
When you've been gone awhile
Bring it home baby
Don't even know how to say maybe
To me
Always see
How I care
We can share
Don't keep your hands to yourself now
Greet me with a wow
Calm me down
I'll turn up your frown
Speed me up next
Like you wrote the text
Call me home and heart
Say I'm so smart
Let me kiss you slyly
Believe of you I think highly
Crown me like a queen
Never be mean
Wrestle me in play
Find me in the fray
Love me
Find the time to hug me
Call me just to say you do
That you never knew
Anyone like me
With me just be
Don't hold back
You're what I lack
Be my fun
Tell me I don't want to run
Love me like I'm paradise
That's it, all concise

Ready, Set, Crash:

I can't stay around and watch this disaster
You're crashing ever faster
You always come first
Didn't notice you treated me the worst
About love you're lazy
And I must've been crazy
Because I could've given you my heart
Just like get ready, set, start
But I made it clear
Forget it, dear

Hitchhikin':

I've stopped fightin'
History on my heels is bitin'
I don't want to wait anymore
What else is this life for?
And where is home now?
No more asking if and how
I wake up screamin' I've found
Silently, but still loud
What does it take to be found?
Blankets fit like a shroud
I've done everything else all the rage
Why do I keep missin' that particular page?
Dined on sushi, shopped at Saks Fifth Avenue
Been boatin' near Mexico too
Been to the top of Empire State
And Southern bourbon in a Southern brick town tastes great
Seen wildflowers stretched under California suns
Now it's kinda like reruns
Walked by old missions' gardens beautiful in the light
And Reno is great at night
Seen horse ranches

New Mexico barren of branches
Giant rocks climbing to the blue Western sky
Yet, why do I sometimes feel like I might die?
I've been everywhere
Except there
I've seen snow on three continents
And seen the stars at night looking out from tents
Had a bonfire on the beach
Why can't I still reach?
I walked through the halls of power
Yet sometimes it's too much to go through an hour
I've hung out with the rich
And I've played perfect from every niche
But where the hell is home when I'm alone in a rush?
Where is the circle of lamp light I can touch?
What do I still look for?
What is missin', everywhere at the core?
I'm just a stranger wanderin' 'round
Seekin' to be found
Hitchhikin' my way through life
On a hypothetical highway of strife

I Won't Do It Anymore:

I won't apologize anymore
I've done it too much
For a heartless holding hush
I looked around and was left like
Something worthless and stupid
While he chases empty-headed shams
While he watches me across the room
While he's holding her hand
While he says there's no passion
He slaps me in the face
I won't let him tell me I'm ugly and mean
I won't let him ignore me while
He sits with the people he uses

And lies to himself that he
Loves her
Because he doesn't
And he didn't
And he never did
And he never has
And he was afraid
And I won't be punished for saying the truth
And he kisses her in their dead rooms
With wilting flowers
And a spit and polish dream
Fixing convenient love at its seams
Never ready for
What he had
And he can keep lying to himself
That she hates him
And that she loves him
And he can sit with her grating on his ears
And he can remember gazing at her in wonder
And he can remember that moment he wanted her
And butterflies down her back
And how he never dared to ask
And he can blame himself
For her fighting
Because he never let her stop crying
And he never apologized for
Letting her alone
And he never got over
Choosing the lesser dream
Choosing lies
And he can lie awake at night
And stop lying to himself?
And he can finally
Stop lying to himself
And can he ever grow up?

It's Okay:

I can't sit and wait
For a double cold hand of fate
I like the sun on my heart
I like much more
I can see a future I want
I like happy secrets
And children laughing in my own living room
And flowers on my breakfast table
And a bold day's kiss goodbye
And eyes so full of love
That your heart is continually turned, looking above
I want a quickened dream
An edge of the cliff stepping out
Voice raising over the dull voices
I want eyes so bright they
My heart set to fire in any light
I want to stop this nightmare
Of worthless days
I want a shameless love
Pouring out in front of everyone
Unafraid of even me
Un-intimidated by nothing that's not there
I want him to save me for his
For us
I want it to be thus
I will walk through life always me
Like balm to the heart I finally know
I was meant for him
Wherever he is
Because he knows the thoughts
I can't say
And the words I do say
He can step past the line
And know it's okay

Did You See Past Your Nothing?:

Can you see past your nothing?
Because I can't anymore
I can't pretend it's not all burned up
I can't care about
Dissolute dead wood
And some shadow of alive
I can't wait for you to stop slapping me
With yourself, your ice-cold hands
Wearing blindfolds
And chasing hollow
Empty-eyed statues
Do they make you feel good
Like other empty things?
Your lies
That paint me up like Satan
Oh paint me up like Satan
And make me into death
And call me a stupid whore
And believe nothing more
You can believe anything you make up
But it won't make it more real
And you won't ever know
The cost
And it was me
You lost
As you continually slap me
With your dead heart

I Woke Up:

I woke up one day and
Gave up everything
For a dream
That turned out to be corrupted and poor
But at least I can say I followed it
I was there in the snow in the rain
And it pressed against my thoughts
But it was wrong
And it was gone
It's not an easy thing to watch
Something you love prove itself
Dust and rats and roaches
And see it turn to poison
To know it was always like
Cobwebs and corruption
And believe it was like the gold fire on the sun
It's no small thing to see admiration
Burn to dust
And tumbleweeds blow across respect
It's hard to imagine there is something
Bright and alive, classy and passionate
And find it dead and dark and blind
It's a sad thing to be wiser
And not to admire anymore
And see a cobwebbed vessel of loss
Where there was a could have been
Something great

He Can't See Past:

He can't see past
Cold and ice burns
He can't see to the nights dark
With the insects buzzing and iced tea glasses clinking
Dark country nights
Honor, shame and a beach bonfire burning
He can't see passion
He can't see Sartre and Anne Frank
And the Federalist Papers running through fingers
He can't see flirting with sex and liberalism
He can't see transgressions I considered and laid to rest
He can't see temptations never honored
He can't see dyed hair colors
And marathons
He can't see me running my hands through the tall grass
He can't see me dancing slow
He can't see me fighting off requests to dance
With music running through our veins
He can't see me fighting off kisses
He can't see reading
Elizabethan lyrics, Marilyn Monroe, Princess Grace or Diana
He can't see my respect for the words of the holy book
He can't see shopping for that dress that was so gorgeous
He can't see me teaching classes
He can't catch my eye
He can't see me tipping a glass of Georgia Peach
Or graduation night by lantern light outside on the beach walk
He can't see dark nights over the ocean
He can't see me in the plane alone
He can't see me trekking through the forest
And he can't see me on the stage, the spotlight around the dark lightlessness
He can't see backstage makeup
And he can't see me cooking tortillas in the warm kitchen
He can't see that housewarming party

Or my friend playing guitar
He can't touch my hand warm
Or hear me talk about how I once believed in that too
He can't see the shiny hardwood floors
Or sit with me by the street holding our drinks and letting the night talk
He can't be honored by my heart
He can't see Napa Valley by noon
Or Los Angeles by night
Or Las Vegas or I-5 so straight all day, all night
He can't know what it's like to be admired like the flowers in the windows
Or the dreams in our air
Or the kings and heroes
He can't fall asleep and know he's safe
He can't cradle his life by his heart and hear his thoughts
Echoed and respected
He can't touch faith and watch from outside the window
He can't watch them raise their glasses as we kiss
He can't cry with joy over an iced cake and a crinkly white dress
Washing over and against him
In the darkened room with all our friends
And he can't see the brightest smiles on their faces
He can't sit at home with me
And when we leave
He can't feel possessive and released
He can't walk alone and feel encouraged as he does
He can't leave his sins on the floor un-remembered
He can't stand on the granite rocks at Yosemite
Or see the reservations in the West
He can't know what it's like to take it seriously
He can't touch another self
He can't finally feel passion above that level
He can't feel anything at all
And he made me feel so small
And I was behind a glass wall
And that was it, that was all
And un-tasted time walks on

What You Wait For:

This perfect world
This clockwork puzzle
Wound up
Time to stop
Don't ask what I didn't know
I knew it; I saw "go"
There were whispers of history in the air
Where she was born, there
Silent for years
How did they all keep silent for years, drawing near?
There's a wonder there
And one day we will care
Did it walk on stage from the dark, from the caves
From wild fields, locusts, honey and knaves?
Did you feel the hand of God, times when it brushed
Human history, so many worlds hushed?
Were you aware
As you stood there
Pages turning in your hand
About the reason and the last stand
Amazing beaches, perfect light
A way beyond this seeming unending night?
There are stars
Wars
What is it for?
Just let your wonder hang there
In this night air
He does care
I can't tell you
What is true
Wonder, words, spoken spirits
Can you hear it?
Knock, find, see

A perfect pearl floating in blackness
Paying a fee for to be free
What you wait for is not less
This perfect, molded, churning mess

Deeply More:

Like you give a damn
While I sit here and cram
Got books stacked to the ceiling
I tell you I'm reeling
Ain't nothin' here
Except knowledge and fear
I studied till I knew it all
Let me tell you, it did not enthrall
Barren of emotion
Like a drug, a sick potion
It makes you think you're livin'
But beware, 'cause it ain't givin'
You could climb to the tallest top
And then, suddenly, watch it stop
I can do it all anytime I want to
But the rest of my life I'd rue
Can't be less than this four wall hell
Recognizin' the toll of the bell
For me
For thee
Knowledge is power rich and big
And a way by which they can all rig
It even brought the atom bomb home like a game
And can bring undying fame
But without what is deeply more
You're still losing forty to four

My Covers:

Oh she is boring
The hell out of you
But you just closed your eyes to
How you coulda had me
Intensity like you thought you'd never see
Her game of offense has got to be trite
Suppose you've never been with a sprite
And mismatched are you
Angered me through and through
That mistake was not light
And you sure won't be with me tonight
And all my very established riches
Thrown back out to that big sea of fishes
I have more bait under my sleeve
And I won't be wasting it on those who leave
And all the money and all the witty lines
Can just go snag somebody who wants deep rhyme
I ain't been sitting here for nothin'
And I was upta somethin'
Demands weren't as high as you thought
I just don't want my love bought
Coulda had that late night candle
Things you can't even be sure you'd handle
I was wantin' to cross the lines again
Like before, way back when
I ain't no loose end
But you didn't even want to tend
I was thinking maybe in a while
Some night you and I would beguile
'Cause I got it all
And under covers could enthrall
You ain't got no idea
Hey baby
See ya
Boy you sure missed the bus

Hope every time you measure what you got tonight
You think of us
And what used to be in sight
What was measurably more right
'Cause every time she touches you now
You'll remember how
It coulda been if you wore me for fashion
And the endless hours of passion
That wouldn't be held back
But you made a new hell; you lack
I hope you're happy with what is so much less
You made your own mess
In your own bed you lie
And in your own mind you deny
Chose what's easy
What's light and breezy
I give it all baby
No more, not even maybe
You got her to take care
And what you reap is fair
And all my charms I'm givin' elsewhere
So there
And I wasn't waitin' long
I was so wrong
You'll never be under my covers
And we'll never be lovers
Don't tell me you wouldn't want it
Don't tell me you weren't lit
To hell with your low standards honey
What you threw away isn't funny

What's to Happen:

What's to happen?
History's banging on the door
I push it shut a little more
The inevitable in this life
Is ready to go
Things start falling down
Lights in the heavens sparkle bright
Sit and stare up at them tonight

Depth:

Intellectual depth is the finest fire
That ever did my soul mire
What I feel and see
A depth beyond me
My enjoyment of life is higher still
I still live deeply and still will
The music, the words, the daring, the risks, the fight
Still looking, still dancing, still believing I might
I drink in life with sureness and a relish sweet and deep
And all my happy tomorrows I reap
Regret never sat long at my door
I want realness, I want more
I will never lie to myself at night
I will never look into eyes that aren't for me right
My heart will never be sold
And I will never be told
What to do
I will never listen except to a higher calling
What I seek is what is true
Sorry that others keep falling
I wouldn't trade my lot in time
For anything that is not mine
I have riches to access that others never know
With every day I turn to go

And walk with a confidence I never lost
And I never need to count the cost
I will have all the things I hope for
All that is rich and more
Love is divine fire, real and living
And my life searches for spirits giving
I have seen so much
But I see that eternal spirit's touch
More wild than they know
Like a traipsing fairy to go
If you could only drink what I drink
And think what I think

Sentinel:

A pale statue
There in the square
Speaking, hands raised
As if on cue
Crumbling buildings gather 'round
It remains unfazed
A sentinel of what's bygone
A last standing vestige of the past
Still marching on
Sometimes I sit in its shade
History to still more fade

Turn My Light On:

Fire
Unswervingly, I just want it to retire
But, it won't so what to do?
Should I just change everything till it's finally through
Me?
I never really thought I'd be a leader again
After I cracked under the overly scheduled strain
But here I go hopping in the fray and changing the world today
Am I finally turning back into who I was?
I can't say
It was a little much to be with someone almost famous
And get screwed over and not be able to see it like Nostradamus
So, I ran 5,000 miles away and then away again
Just picked up and left back then
And the same old story I chose
This really blows
So, I guess I get to turn it on, flip on the switch
Have you ever seen me choose to light up the room?
Yah, there's a hitch
It's completely fake, but no one can tell
They think I'm just so freakin' swell
I've had it off for years and years
Tryna conquer my other-wordly fears
You're gonna catch me out on Saturday night
I'm not sure whether or not it's right
And who knows if I'll be good or not
I always have been, but sometimes I think it lots
Of shades of pointless
Why not just be a mess?
Okay, flip on the switch
We'll see if I can carry this out without a hitch
And forget the aches inside me
Cause if you don't feel anything, you're finally free
So, don't be surprised if you hear I made it big
It's just my own personal little dig

At myself for never trying, never believing
Waiting for dying
If you turn yourself on like a lamp
Suddenly the whole world wants to camp
It's a frightening thing and sometimes people lose their souls
That way, 'cause inside there's nothing but lots of great big holes
If you already lost those important dreams
There's just nothing it seems
To lose that can kill you
Oh sure you still want things, you do
And you care and you work and you're tryna be good too
But you really know you have nothing to lose, nothing to fear
Going through life without a care
Maybe there will be regrets
But I can't sit here and let
This bother me
I have to run away
Can't you see?
If you turn yourself on like a light
Are you really still always alone at night?
Even if someone ends up forever next to you?
'Cause you have so much fun, you do
Do you still think of the moon you couldn't bring down
When you're dancing your way through town?
I'll turn my light on if it dulls the pain
At least they'll know and like my name

Kiss Me, Sunshine:

I was holding my baby's little hand
And I was sitting picking flowers
I was walking over the sand
After our wedding day
And I was writing by your side
And I was sitting on the cliff
Dangling my feet over
Giggling, laughing too much

And I was grocery shopping with my king
And I was making dinner
In the fire light
And I was sitting on dew-painted grass
And I was on the porch
The evening setting in
And there was never a
Kiss with and without desire so real
Or a moment so relaxed
He let it all past
He sewed up the seams
He took a step
They never dreamed
And there was happiness
For the first
For the last
And he knew there was a cause
For which he'd stumble and
For which he'd live
And she was not
At all that much
Difficult
And there was no keeping it
From off her face
And there was no keeping it
From off his face
And neither one was lying
When they were walking side by side
A quiet forgiveness
A rain-drenched fire
A rightness
An abiding desire
A never quenched fire
What is right
Is always different
When you are near it

To Touch God's Face:

This bed is so damn lonely
Why should I save it for you only
How will I do what I please
If it's on my mind
Then, I'm still a tease
God would forgive me
Otherwise insanity will be
So how then does perfect save me?
You're late
You never found me
Maybe for all my grace
A tomb-ful life is my fate
Oh sanctimonious judges who can see
I played your game
But this is no big deal
And that's a shame
I did more right than you've done
That could be
Life is more
Than a sanctimonious shun re-run
Their spirits themselves they can't restore
I believe
And this is light
And nothing more
A sin among the pantheon of sins slight
With God our poor souls unite
To no hell, no dark place
But to touch God's face
Sin is sin
Why not let me in?

Seer:

Take down your mask
I'm takin' you to task
Quit lyin' to me
You know I could always see
You've gotta go stall
With dreams that tall
You ain't got no secrets baby
And you're not lookin' for what may be
But what will be and should be

The Unexpected Arrow:

The gods are smiling at me
Let it be
Fortune rains like a glittering torrent
You are more it
Than anyone
And I'm having far too much fun
You light me
Set the match
Let it catch
I'll let it be
'Cause it's gonna go
Well, what - I didn't know?
Makes it all so
Enticing, entrancing, intense with light
Oh, it feels so good not to fight
Look what's around this corner now
Where did it come from, how?
Steal me, thrill me
Let the fever chill me
Stake a moment's little soul on that
While all alone I sat
Somewhere bells were ringing
And whimsical birds were singing
And now they found me, shocked me
Wowed me times three
What, can timeless wonder me enhance?
Oh thrill me, catch my winking soul while
You and I dance
Here on this departing tile
What is floating on the air
When you realize I'm still standing there?
And when we caught on
To each other like dew-dropped dawn
We were long gone in love
Unexpected happy arrow from above

I Had a Heart Too:

What made you into the devil?
It was never on the level
You were a step away from God yesterday
But you walked away
You were like dry ice
You can't even be partially nice
You were never there
You didn't care
And now you're blaming me
For blowing up, letting it free
You know you deserved it
I took a hit
You think it's everyone else's fault and you're always right
That's why everyone else walked away with a fight
They just didn't want to be stepped on
Tell me, how is that wrong?
What's wrong with saying what I feel?
It was surreal
You wouldn't care if the rest of the world died
I guess when someone's always lied
That's how it goes
And his callousness grows
You would hear me crying
You wouldn't be caught dead trying
So if I told you what I think of you
Tell me is that any crueler than being screwed?
Don't blame me
You can see
You might as well have slapped me
Laughed, you'd let me die
I don't know why
You never gave a damn
And lied when it came down to telling me I am
Someone sweet to you
I just feel screwed
You left me hanging in limbo

And you know
You couldn't even be a bad friend
All you ever did was rend
So if I said mean things to you
Think of me on my knees cryin'
It's not just you, I have a heart too
And you're undependable and lyin'
With friends as there for me as you
Enemies would be better company, it's true
I tried and tried and all I met was lyin' ice
You're deluded if you think you were nice
I would have given you anything
When I talked to you my heart would just sing
I would have been the most loyal friend
But you shut me out while I cried and let me rend
You couldn't take a second to offer one part
While I would have given any section of my heart
So if I used words that scorched you
Don't forget, I had a heart too
And I adored you

The Dissident:

I've been savin' face
Gotta restore grace
Seeing what I shouldn't see
Losin' what I wanna be
Dyin' for gettin' there
Too late to prepare
Gotta take this test
Have to go against the best
Jumpin' in feet first
Tell me I've seen the worst
Makin' dreams out of despair
Not ready to land nowhere
Stunning the world by placin' bets
When they were makin' sure to send regrets
But I'm the one with the big plans now
Even though it looks like I've gone under
Before you can blink twice and ask how
I'll have set the status quo asunder
I'm about to steal your thunder
Before you will say go
I'll have marshalled all I know
The establishment
Will be spent
And though it will never repent
I'll have set up my dissent to the proper extent
To cause it all
To crash and fall

Let's Split:

Tinkerbell
Or Jezebel?
Care to tell
Why you think you know me so well?
Walking by the ocean, waves crashin'
Cupid's chasin' me like an assassin
Taking off for the nightlights of Egypt
Oh . . . I think I might have slipped
And I don't think I'm so equipped
To just ignore
How damn much I adore
You and your infernal magic spell
Leads down the road where?
I don't care to tell
I'm takin' off for Manhattan's nightlife and fashion
Trying to forget about passion
And then maybe Rio will bring me
Farther and really guarantee
I won't wander back
Won't get off track
I got all my defenses
And you've got your expenses
I don't think I'll let cupids arrow track down its target
So, baby, why don't we just split?

Baby I Can:

I ain't got no love
When push comes to shove
Just gotta resign
You got me puttin' calamine
On the sting
I ain't so up for
This goodbye thing
And one more kiss
Before you shut that door
You're leavin' me amiss
But baby I can handle this

Spike It Up:

The world can be dark
And utterly stark
Is there more beyond that chapter?
Is this a factor?
Is there yet more?
Beyond this door?
What time is it?
How do I fit?
Spike up the punch
I have a hunch
What do I do
When it comes to what's not true?
Where is the scale
By which I measure?
And when do I bail?
And what price for pleasure?

Smoldered Ice:

Forsaken
And not taken
Banned from high intensity
Disallowed to partake of the propensity
Cold and smoldered
Cracked like ice
Tossing it like dice
Sold by time
Stuck with rhyme

Watchin':

That's some kind of desire
Don't even think about setting me on fire
Take a step back
I mean it, cut me some slack
Your eyes make me shake
So let's not fall in love
It's gotta be some kind of mistake
We gotta get ahold of
Ourselves okay?
I'm not used to this kind of disarray
Let's go to page one
Pretend nothing's begun
I really don't know what to do
So, I hope you're watchin' you

Hush:

Diamonds fall from the sky
When I think of it
I perpetually die
And yet I sit
Still and think
Always on the sweetest brink
Got my candle
Got my flame
More than anyone can handle
Too much to tame
Light up the room in the dark
From the depths of what's stark
Lift up the light
In the darkest, loneliest night
Hush the candle's on
It's almost dawn

Fast:
You're just bein' nice
I ain't got no dice
Been driving in this one lane
So long, I've gone insane
Pull over by the beach now
Walk through the sand now
I've got a box of matches
I'll light the fire, hope it catches
Got a bonfire
Got my satire
Let's talk about the past
Ain't got nowhere to go fast

Watching Them Walk:

Sunday, sittin' there
Eyes locked in a come hither stare
Takes her hand
It's just never bland
Get out and go for a walk
Maybe just sit in the sun and talk
He's gotta admit
She's got him all lit
Got all the fellas emulous
Seeing him and her thus
Got all the ladies dishing
Gossiping, wishing
But is it a backlit show
Or a true love glow?

Ain't Nothin' Wrong:

Prim and proper
Doesn't let that stop her
Nightingales and morning coffee before sunrise
Burning both ends
Helps make amends
Flying through the day
Always gotta have her say
But he's got one up on her
That spitfire just starts to concur
When he turns that sweet charm on
She's his pliant pawn
And she says there ain't nothin' wrong
When you're where you belong

Cinnamon Trouble:

Oh it's like cinnamon
It's like sundaes
It's like an escalade expedition
It's like maraschino cherries
Little lightning bug fairies
Dancing through the room
It's wild and wrong
And right all along
It's like flowers spilling over the spread
And being dead, but realizing you're still alive
It's fun like fake danger
Scientific like a heat exchanger
Ooh we could get in so much trouble
And then go and redouble
Never seen that wild side
Think I'm about sick of missing that ride

Brushing Away the Butterflies:

Fluttering around in her head like a butterfly, her other thoughts scatter
She wishes this wasn't the matter
Senselessly, she feels like a funny wallflower
Even though she's well aware she has boxed up star power
It's really hard to believe
When it comes down to love
You'd have to hit her over the head
To make her perceive
Or even believe
She's supposed to receive
So, sometimes she would get that dreamy-eyed look
But before you know it cynicism came and took
Love and all its silliness away
Before her thoughts would get too far astray

And it suits her, she found
Because generally she's always wrong
And she gets left standing on their common ground
Just a little too far along
With no one to whom she does belong
And so she's scared
And always makes sure she's unprepared
Never notices love declared
Remains frozen but spared
She thinks it's better to ignore
Frozen to the core
Than be wrong like she was before
And she clings to it more and more
And she brushes away the butterflies
Deeply terrified that they're always going to be lies

Not a Prize:

Contrary
Entirely wary
Also reckless and feckless
She's all over the place
In a glass case
She's a doll
No she's a ball
Kick her around
Fun will abound
She can't recall
What it's like outside the cell wall
If she was made of porcelain that could shatter
Would, to them, it matter?
Do you worship a lily?
Or do you stomp it silly?
It's always about you
But, she, they can't construe
Fire up the lame debut
Constantly they pursue

Does neglect come with a receipt?
Just like it comes packaged all complete?
Back for a repeat?
While, her, they delete?
Consideration
Is a sorely missed sensation
They get in line
But the shrine
Doesn't feel particularly divine
Always on the receiving end of design
And happiness no chance to shine
Do her shoulders break
When all they do is take?
They're always pulling the wool
Over her eyes
What would she give for one thoughtful
Without disguise, no more lies,
No surprise, always tries
Who can surmise?
Who is so wise?
Never treats her like a prize
Who hopes for no goodbyes
Loves her till she dies

Flatter, Flatter, Fall:

It's no matter
Go ahead and flatter
You think those people notice me?
You think appearance is the key?
There're always those much more pretty
And so very many who are tons more witty
Do you really think I get what I want?
And that I'm really very nonchalant?
You think I'm sitting on top of the world?
You think all my wings are unfurled?
I've learned I'm really kind of minuscule

Practically a molecule
There are a billion more beautiful
A billion givers more bountiful
A billion personalities more delightful
I've very little to be boastful of
I've learned it's a terrible fumble
Not to be a great deal humble
Appearances can be deceiving
And that's an important thing
For me to keep perceiving
I haven't always got sang-froid
Pride before the fall
That's about it, all and all

Well What Do You Know?:

I'm so glad we said goodbye
Because all you ever did was make me cry
Though it's been years
I've only just managed to mop up the tears
When I was looking at you
Did I miss
Somebody real, somebody true?
What did I ever see there?
All it ever led was nowhere
I'm so glad you're just a friend now
Though how it got here I can't say how
But I don't think of you much, ever
Except when I get a brief letter
It's nice to know I've long had my heart back
Totally whole, hasn't even got a crack
My dreams are unrelated to you now
Well what do you know - wow

This Moment in Time:

The rules we've swept behind us
The dangers we've faced
We're so brave, aren't we?
I live for now, and the last day
I cherish this moment now
And yesterday sings for joy
With this my muse
But how do I find I want to freeze
This moment in time?
This moment is every moment
And every moment is this moment
So come and dance with me
Let's go dance
Let's go and run by the ocean
To clasp hands and run in the dusk
Dreams are a poor fabric to weave
One's life up of
Like an enchanted weaver
On a magical loom
I dream a little dream for now
And I have this twinkle in my eye
Because what is the next day and
The last day?
I know today
And you know today
It's just one long, long, short day
So, come and weave our tomorrows
I reach towards no fable
Because if I have reached today
The next day is today
I will be there
Come away and sit underneath the dark pines
With me in the daylight, in the dusk
Lay back with me on the damp grass
And smell time with me

And let us think of everyone who has ever stared at the moon
It makes us feel small
And then we get afraid
Tossing out on that boat in the big, lost ocean waves
And the rush of now
Tells me just how I want to leave
I want to leave and float up to the moon
Living while I am alive to live
Living tomorrow is a shabby gilded gloss
So, my daring bold dreamer
Let's sweep away all our tomorrows
And come live with me now
I dare you to dance with me till our shoes wear out
I dare you to fight with me till there
Is not one more weapon in our armament
I dare you to speak with a vivacious tongue
I dare you to weave a legacy
To top that of sunshine in Rome
To be as loving
As a momma coaching a little babe to walk
Honey, come and live dreams with me
And let us dance to the finish line
And fight the hand of death
And leave our little whispers in their hearts
Come and let us go live forever

Darkened Seats:

Life is no stage
A center to gravitate to
An enchanted circle
Under the lights
The actors trip across the stage
In a world of magic and lies
Always something beautiful
Lovely sadness, fearful, frightful
Touching passion

So fine and in fashion
People seek it out
To sit and sink it in
To watch and wonder
In the dim off-stage light
They seek it out in their own silent nights
The excitement, the crazy love, the pretty plights
Beckon and call
As if either cast
Or
The ever-enchanted, ever-enthralled
Were living it all

How, When Will It Get Me?:

Beautiful woman
With time to spend
Loved and comforted
Alive and kissed
Smart and joli
Blessings that would dearly be missed
Are held on the end of a puppet's string
Bid to follow a whim
And I am the puppet
On the end of a string
And great is the power
Who plays with the wind
That may tangle my strings
And who is it that dangles my delicate dreams?
Fearful is this
To be a plaything
Just like the wind
Who's sent to break things
And stirs the graveyard of 'tlantis
Unpredictable thing
Does your master
Catch all my prayers

And follow my cares?
My flowery debutante ball
Will it be blown soon into dusk?
And will the candles be snuffed?
Will my life last as long
As one way the wind may blow?
Or will the eye of the sea
Merrily traveling
Come and grab me?

Every Day Enchanting:

I have never loved anyone so much
I have never so wanted to touch
I have never seen tomorrow in eyes
Till I saw tomorrow in his eyes
I have heard that hearts can break
But I don't want to take
I don't need more
I don't have a care to take score
So, if there's a loss
It can't very much cost
It's content
And it's not
It's a high stakes game to lay
A heart on the table and let it stay
It's true
I really am so very sought
But with him, the world is new
I can color up my tomorrows
With dreams of him
And that can't be bought
Like something you can't bottle, the feeling
Hangs in the air
I can't help but care
In me, in me here
There's a place, there's home in his eyes

I can't help but surmise
That though this keeps getting better
He doesn't love me
Somewhere there is a still better man
Who knows he hasn't met her
I can't wander like a wild dream forever
There is a freedom I can sometime sever
In aspirations stay hearts living
Join with me in this spirit of giving
Really love like dandelions chasing atoms dancing
Walk down the street, but across oceans
Everyday enchanting

He:

He found me
What I couldn't see
Became all my dreams
Unscripted me at the seams
I was caught in-between the lines
In-between our stares
What a sweet dream we share
Don't you dare
But you do
You do, and I do care
I'm swept off my feet
Every time our eyes meet
I can't control what I don't know
I can't understand
Why you really do want to be my man
I don't want you to go
You seem to love me so
I take cautious steps under your adoring eyes
Am I really your first prize?
I can't imagine a better place than in your arms
Your soft words have an arresting charm
You are like Eden in my life

I cannot believe you asked me
What a heaven-issued decree
It's like dew-painted kisses
To know I'll be your Mrs.
I am lost when you walk beside me
In a world of joy, a feeling so free
You never felt better, you say
Every day you find some richer way
To love me more
And I, you, adore
Mi amor
My sweet armor and my shield
You can't even stand the thought
Of playing the field
I'm all the wrapped-up worlds you sought
I love you
I love you
I love you too

Fame:

Candy-coated lemon drops
Tinsel tops
Picture perfect
Glitzy props
Photo image
Freaks circle
Critics are the hurtle
Spotlight steals the starry sky
Bended magic
Broken fabric
Brightly woven up
Is my embroidered stage
Into a suitcase cage
Flitter
Flitter
Wave and pan
The camera lost its favorite fan

Dying Young:

Don't let this life I live so free
Go down in pain that should not be borne
Meaningless to be
Tell me you love me
When new maidens
Careless walk
On my grave
Will you never think of these
Once un-faded locks?

Attention:

Attention I crave
From my barren destitution
Who are we walking through air
If there is no one there
To touch, wonder, doubtlessly care?
No one to know who we are?
We exist alone
If we exist unknown

The Belly:

So, I walked in the belly of poetry
And everything not one meaning had
How sweet, how unique, how complete
A partner for all
As Eve from Adam
And Adam for Eve
A coat to a sleeve
A day for a night
A moon for a sun
An "I've none"
For "Got some"
An elevation underground
A theatre-in-the-round
A little here; a little there
A crazy meaning hanging in the air

Despair:

Death is at the doorstep
Lurking in the shadows
Sighing, hoping, dreaming
Waiting to take me off
It matters not if it is now
Or if it is then
So why pretend it's okay
To pretend about things?
Lying is what we all do best
Lying about who we love
Lying about how we feel
Lying about what we need
Lying in actions
Lying, cheating, crying
Breaking, hating, dying

Hymn of Religion:

Soft, dreamy eyes
Always up and in the sky
Lifting, tilted twin pools of life
Staring, waiting
Always a little strange
A little far away
Staring into blue, lofty fields
Such blessings, such favors!
Hidden away
In the heart of a maid
She waited
She knew
They did not perceive
But still a virgin did conceive

Constant:

Oh you are my constant
When all the world
Runs circles around my brain
And dizzy I become
The world can't compete
When you kiss me till I can't feel
Can't hear
The empty streets' bustling appeal
You touch me till the bills float
Away with all the other sum of my cares
Like the ocean surf that breaks
Onto the shore
In my soul
When your skin like a feather brushes mine
And the baby never cried
When you show you love me
By doing the dishes
I'm a mirthful woman

When you tease my soul
By winking as you hold my coat
Bless me heaven for I have sinned
I love a heart of solid gold
My constant prince
In the past, present, and future tense

Less Me:

If I had been loose with my words
And given light rein to this my sacred vessel
It would not have been hard for you to ask me
But then you would not have loved me
Others who did not love me
Nor respected this sacred vessel
Have not found it hard to ask me
To them a light crime it would have been
To injure this light step
To you
Any ungentle action, look, or thought
Would be likened to profane or speak blasphemy
Your eyes would watch my step in your view
And wished ever to watch my step
In caressing other women
You found your mind could wander
In lightly grabbing my hand to apologize
For some silly misstep
It was found it
Could feel like ice melting, tingling, touching your
Soul alive
Your kindness surpassed
The highest efforts and gifts bestowed upon me
By men who earnestly sought my hand
But you sought my spirit, my soul, all my days
Even to age and you saw yourself
And all your future's moments safely kept
In a friend, a pilgrim who delved

As deep into you as you prayed
I would ever go
But this love seemed undercurrent
To be voiced would open a dam
That never could ever be shut
We sought to open it
But who can help but be frightened by
Prospects of a flood
Still we sought to dwell with the ocean
You left still dreamy
For angels don't fall from heaven
To live with men
Do they?
And scared
As of an apparition or real angel
You stared into my eyes
The skies I am supposed to dwell in
Are not always fluffy, baby blue, and crisp white
You left your angel fighting the lightening that struck
When as a man spooked by a spirit
You took leave of my acquaintance without telling me
It was not for a little while
But for all the rest of my life
And I thought we were just saying goodnight
So, I wasn't to see you where I always saw you anymore
If I bothered to ask I would know where you were
But what mattered was that you didn't bother to ask
Your eyes always set a kick of new life to my soul
Pity you did not set it in me as well
And set me beside you always to dwell
If I had been different
You would not have found it so difficult to tell me
But if I had been different
You would not love me till forty past forty past twenty

Guessing Wrong:

I have nothing to remember you by
But the feeling in my heart
The pictures in my head
The worn, cornered memories
I try not to think of you
Because if I delve too deep into the waters
I cry salt to tease my wounds
I wish you would know
With all my heart
I would have given the answer yes
Why didn't you just ask me?
In my room, on my knees I begged God for you to stay
Just a month, two months, just forever
And you stayed
And then I watched you leave
With not one more thing accomplished
And all left unfinished
I felt I played the fool
And I knew I was a jester
Because you didn't love me
Because I had to watch you leave
In your simple action
You wrote volumes
And I read the piercingly cool and honest words
In the moment of clearest insight
Within wisdom's sorrow I did rightly see
The feeling of ocean deep infinity
The carouses of soft attraction
Were thrown into a hurricane of fear
I buried my softest hope
That should never have been born
Buried alive
All of a sudden
A mourner many times
But feeling like a widow now

Why did this misstep miss its mark so well
As to bury itself in hell
In snow-covered ground, all white?
My hope that was discarded once too much
Is spent
I bought deep love for a high price
For a fool's gold I spent my riches lavishly
On a high-risk runner
I, who have loved often have never loved so dear
Expensive was the toll you took
I played the guesser again
Happily misled by playful eyes
Wildly I placed my bet
And you won I guess

Did You Ever?:

Now you're here telling me that all those years
You were thinking of me and in love sincere
With my words, the dream of me, my face
And you want me to believe that was really the case
You ran into me and your eyes said it all
You could never hide; I saw you fall
I know that, but can you think it was easy?
What am I supposed to be made of?
I wanted someone to need me
I wanted you to say you were in love
I would start a fight in my frustration
At least then I could express something
Not be lost, fighting a trembling sensation
My feelings I would never mention
First
And your rejection was the worst
You told yourself it was too much trouble
And your efforts to not be in love set on redouble
Do you really believe the comforting picture you paint of me
As not at all what a few times you thought you could see?

Do you ever wake up and see through the haze?
Do you ever realize you shut yourself up in a maze?
Were you ever afraid there was one woman who would leave you breathless?
Come on now, confess
Were you ever hanging on to a vision that you couldn't
That I was poison and all the wrong things and you shouldn't?
Did you ever get wounded by a too tart tongue
But find yourself, far below the surface
Wishing you'd won and we'd just got along?
Did you ever wonder if there was a way out of the mess?
Did you ever wonder if the fire that did so inspire
Would actually keep burning?
Did you ever bother to desire?
Did you ever think outside your infuriating box
That you shut up with four-thousand double locks?
Did you ever just sit and be near her and drop the cynicism?
Did you ever grab hold of the colors from her prism?
Did you ever take the biggest chance, the chance you could let something matter?
Did you ever risk telling her and wonder if you'd wake up, if you really had her?
Did you ever tell yourself it was cobwebs and noxious cyanide
But deep down know it was harmless, like a little kid's amusement ride?
Did you ever find yourself waking up with an empty ache?
Did you ever wonder if you killed love for your own sake?
Did you ever feel completely inadequate
Like a crazy guy out on the make?
Did you ever wonder if there was one woman who really
Was everything you thought, every dream
A safe place in the melee?
Doesn't this poem just make you want to scream?
Why don't you close your mouth and take my hand?
I think then we'd understand
Each other, just a little bit at first
Or is it you can't think of anything worse?
Did you ever realize what you were and are and want?

Did you ever just want to be blunt?
Did you ever want to walk out of the fighting, the mist?
Did you ever think there would be another first time you were kissed?
Did you ever lay your entire heart on the line?
Did you ever wonder what was really in mine?
Did you ever want a home with a friend, with a burning fire?
Did you ever think you could so much desire?
Did you ever have some faith?
Were you always so wary of a possible mistake?
Did you ever want to make amends?
And think it would just be the ten thousandth time
And you'd have to watch the dream rend?
Well I'm
Really not that cold or that crazy
Maybe you should have got to know me

Mem'ries:

Did I ever love you?
Sitting cross-legged on my bed
I remember and I see
Dimly lit shadows
In a strange dance before me
Past shaded walks and paths
Birthday cakes
And empty, busy everydays
I see a rose-colored cheek
And a soft whispering night
As I glided with you
On airy feet
In the glowing, dim light
And I remember a match struck
And a wax-molded dream lit too bright
Were you and I really together in that young night?
I am here in beige satin splendor
Beside me is he

The one who made me forget all my dreams
How wild were we!
How fearless and free!
Driving around in your classy car
You took me everywhere
My partner we were there
I remember the first note
That last glance
The pink roses
And buried in my childhood photos
Are those brazen poses
When the bud of beauty
Lit the dawn of my first life
You took my hand
And we danced through class
Through summer
Through swimming and parties
Through all of my remembered life
From the first shy, sly glance
To the last careless goodbye
You and I were side by side
Tonight I sit and shudder
And a little wind blows at the candle
Through the open window
And the white curtains lick at the inside of my bedroom
And remind me of how you stole me away
To dance in the light of the moon
Or was it on the moon?
And I think I still have not left you
My spirit must love it, being with you
For I see us together, holding hands
On the green, whistling lawn
You smiling and I in my red sundress
Why did you not remember to take the rest of me
When you went away through the Valley
And over the dale to sit in the moon?
You left a pale, tipsy shell
Being greedy you took all my memories

All of my remembered life is with you
And you could not leave my heart here on Earth
But took it away with you
And we went tripping over the stormy clouds
You wanted to go and dance with me on the moon
Someday I too will join with me and you

Reputation:

Tell them all you know
Run her into the ground
Give them a good show
Don't let her rest
Don't even let her go
Rack her from head to foot with fever
Make her blush
When she hears your taunts
She doesn't know
How you could possibly say so
Throw her to the wolves
Haunt her in the church
Chase her on the road
Crowd in on her little form
Throw firebombs
While she has set to pray
Send heralds to announce her wickedness
Set her in chains
Try to put her in prison
But there is not a chain
There is not a cell
There is not a way
To enslave
That little form
Lock up her liberty
And she will tell you
I see not how you say you have won
Can you not see that I
Am absolutely, completely, utterly still free?

The Subway:

I caught sight of your face
On a subway train gliding by
And when you were
Far gone ahead on your path
It was there
The dream of you
Hovering in the air
Could that be real?
That scent of something lingering
On my hair
On my clothes
It's like I know
The taste of you
The touch of you
The scent of you
But I have not yet been there
What is left here lingering?
Is it the sense of expectation
Mingling, shouting, lingering
In the busy subway station?
Has fortune snuck up on me?
Will it too need some fare?
What does it mean?
What will I pay
Till I see that face again?
And like a flash
Of fleeting philosophy
The little cluttered moment was gone
Years later
In the lobby of some shabby theater
Electric blood suddenly pulsed through me
How mysterious that
You and I met that day
Years later
The memory that could never fade

And now we are un-swayed
Together
Today, every day,
You and I play
Caught up in each other
Vowed to stay

You and I:

Timeless, searching gaze
Met mine
And I broke free
As if by stepping out of a lightless maze
Had I been a woman gliding
In a hoop skirt
Through festooned halls
Or tear-stained, starving
Clutching rags and tatters
In a place, a world
Un-heedful, hateful of law
I trust even if I had
Grown up in the shadow of Pharaohs
In a land of deadened, crumbling monuments
A maiden drawing water at a well
I would find you still
I'd leave this vessel beside by earthenware jar
At the water's edge
And even if the Sea of Forgetfulness
Tried
From me, you, she could not pry
They say love is blind
But ghosts have a way that they see
So this way will come to me
For the space between atoms
They learned
Sends forth fire to find ashes
Of nature left here

And if nature, the synonym of death,
From that place can be conquered
Then we, when we go,
To walk around atoms
There we will be
You with me
Unceasing, unhampered, cut free

Doubtless:

Beyond doubt or reason
Rhyme or myth
I love you
Searching your eyes
Brought the only answer I ever want
To my only question
So, existence in that second was satisfied
And verified and
Justice touched her hand to mine
I see you, seek you
Beseech you
You hold my future up
Like my dreams hold up
The banner of the starry dark
Velvet sky
Bleed me, burn me, bury me
And still the fragrance of your
Spirit will carry me
I live, I thrill,
I die
Completely, utterly, satisfied

Love at Armageddon:

The colors
They went out of the sky
Pines are pasty, old, wretched
Butterflies are moths
The bluebirds fade into the sky
And does no one sing anymore?
I cannot see
So much I cry
An olive branch
This dusty place
Did proffer me
It shone and glimmered
Dew dropped from its leaves
And golden sun lit its separate seams
I, blinded by my greed,
Grabbed hold the lovely thing
And angels enfolded me in their wings
The birds twittered through dusty night
Like as if 20,000 yellow candles
Illuminated chapels near heaven
And vocal turned in flight
Like fireworks' foot soldiers
Sang a battle hymn
To all the world's skies bereft of night
And I saw a flimsy rope snap
And that beautiful vision
Was left imprinted in prism's colors
Screaming, I called for all the others
All this bright, golden light
So warm, so seductive
In the luminous, beautiful,
Balmy aura of its lovely colors
Of gold
It was so hard to determine
I snatched to my possession

A sickly vine
Not a luscious fruit's home and repine
Does love so often steal all of rhyme?
Why before me has everything
Acquiesced
The thin layer of dust
It won't come off
And all around this crater there is nothing
Where have all the colors gone?
Dim, dim, dim
Still, always
Where did this light originate itself at?
It cannot be in my eyes
But there is nothing left
To light the dust off the blasted pit
Light the dusky paint of coming night
Away
I wander
Why, why, why do I
See no more light?
Put back the colors
Bring me back my delight
Shadows crawl and wrestle
Before me
Men beg and fight and hate
Tricked, the one I love and I came too late

I Wish You Would Love Me:

I wish you would love me
But you won't
And for all of myself I've given
You don't
And still Heaven's door is hidden
When I just can't reach
And you just won't wait
And I'm the one time still can't teach
I guess I really can't change fate
And though those wiser, more sane will preach
Still the image of you I see scintillate
And I know I'll never mind that you're out of reach

Settling:

Come and start a fire with me
In the temple
Come and start a moment
In our memory book
Come and fill our picture book
With pages of happy smiles
Come and leave a legacy
Come and weave a legacy
With me
Come and share my hearth
Come and dream your dreams
In the place we'll always meet
Come and leave those winking women all behind
Come and build a bond
Your house, sweetheart
Has been like a revolving door
But I know that just
Isn't what's inside a beating heart
Come and find a reason to

Jump and not to jump
Love gets left standing a wallflower
When those women love you
'Sides what is being LOVED?
So, I hear
You're a lover?
Just let me whisper here
Some good advice
Love, by definition,
Is felt inside you
Those women aren't inside you
So, I hear
You're a lover
Is something wrong?
You look a little sick
Don't tremble so
Well, you could leave
And leave the ember in the arctic
Or . . . you could stay
Leave all your projects at bay
Share your name
Nurture a flame
I wish you would
Come, let me whisper in your ear
Today, tomorrow, and forever
Yes, yes
I dare ya

How Can You Not?:

How can you not love me?
I turned down those
Groping, heartless, loveless
Exhaustless princes
They're piled in heaps
In the I'm-not-moved
Category
Of my motion-picture memory
My hair is shaped
In piles of satin poetry
I carry myself in the
Pattern of years of passionately loved ballet
Momma's tummy molded me after classic statuary
Unfortunately, with you I might as well be
For all the attention you pay me
I thought my looks would touch you
I like to hide cozy under pages of wit and wonder
And I've drunk in pages of silver-tongued, medaled words
From the moment I could toddle along till now
I thought my wit would touch you
I try, but I can't get you
I laugh so much
My jokes, my jokes, my jokes
Don't they even turn your heartless head?
Crazy man!
I have waited all my life
For the attention of someone I respect as much as you
For the attention of someone I respect as much as you

Beauteous Man:

He was handsome when I knew him
My momma said he'd bartered his soul to hell
For a countenance like that
For which, to my unsleeping, never-ceasing sorrow, I fell
From my pedestal
All for some talk of roses and daisies and oaths sworn to heaven
To my shame I was captured, my vision lay beaten and hazy
Thinking, gawd, to send back to God this sweet baby
That man was so comely and fair
A rich jewel with none who could compare
And time swirled thickly, forgivingly near me, around me,
Sweet love, its gone through me
I loved him, oh yes
I did love him
But worry not, my life-painter, I'm true
That man whom I knew
He's not handsome, but sadly bent under some quite
Transparent weight, curly locks thinned, tired, and grey
So, I see, in some such similar state are we
But, I, unlike him, do not chase for a subject, a fan
An onlooker, an admirer, a sham
I, spurned and unloved, took my baby and ran
Who would ever have known I'd find such a beautiful, beautiful
man

My Roses and My Wine:

Roses and romantic wine glasses
Grace the table as I see
For the first time in all my time
Into the very sweetness of all my dreams
The promise of all my tomorrows
Staring back at me with life
Through eyes of ink black
That write my life with the candle
Iridescent glow of his spirit's
Concentration on me
As I am thoroughly caught up in loving him
Completely

So I Wait:

The rain pounds outside the window
I miss you; I miss your spirit
I sit in despondence and my faculties are a prey to fancy
I stare till I see no more of the immediacy
I see into golden, sun-kissed streets, barren of tears
I see a life planned long ago
When our hearts met
Our spirits became like flesh and started
When in the crowds, touch without sense
Words without speech, sight without seeing
Were the best of communications
Intuition, sight to the inner spirit, racked that day's mundane expectation
I recognized in you, you recognized in me,
Kinship without sin
At once and for the first time
I saw the road my life would take,
The path my feet would step to,
The song my soul would sing to

For all the rest of my life
Pre-knowledge bid me to be fascinated with you
And caught my hands up
And bound them to the sense of you
And chained me to your memory
Bless me God, for I am lacking now
And I hazard I will know him again one day
I hazard all I have
To gain all I have
I see the day of days
I see spiritual movement
The locks break
I open the door, step through into airy sunshine
I see your true image
My longer hair, my glowing skin
You lift me up, onto my prancing, neighing white horse
And you and I would ride on
White horses through the meadow glen

In Lebanon:

I know your world
Was torn with war
And the glittering minions of death
Exploded in your homeland
On your door step
And I saw you
Where the women wailed
What world is this?
This globe hurtling through time
Where you watched a baby die
And the guns shattered silent night
I see you screaming
To insanity
To a people whose vision ran red
I can see it in you
Somewhere below the surface

Buried back long ago
When you lost your faith
How glad I am
I took you into my world
And burned away
The foundations of the past
And the echoes of every last terrifying sound
And you found in me energetic
Serenity
You said
All the world could burn itself to hell
But that you had found springs of faith in me
That I, myself, could quell those flames
But one flame I couldn't ever touch
The flame of us
Because you, whom I love, love me so much

Optimism:

Whispered tension
From ghosted voices
'Membered in my intuition
Memories fear not to tread
My choices let me not to bed
Lifeless love's a pretty trick
Undying vows burn
But time can snuff the longest wick

Fleeting:

Life is fleeting
Goodbye is always close at hand
And cold, stone monuments stand
To hearts stopped beating
. . . What might have been
If not by one step you'd seen
Or not had one chance meeting
Life's curtains, they fall fast
Generations slip by, under one sun
And even this, today, is soon the past
And every sweet moment, though you try to make it last
You see, yourself, you're still only one
And even this now, today, is soon the past.
Gone will be we, now the cast
And my writer's story then is done
I put down my pen at last.

Index of Poems

Ain't Nothin' Wrong.	118
Already Given.	87
Animated, Not to Be Blamed:	55
Attention.	129
Awed.	47
Baby I Can.	115
Bands of War.	7
Bar Sense.	42
Bare Floors.	59
Beauteous Man.	148
Brushing Away the Butterflies.	119
But I Just Don't Want It To.	83
Christmas Morning.	40
Cinnamon Trouble.	119
Constant.	131
Crazie.	52
Cross.	49
Darkened Seats.	124
Deeply More.	100
Depth.	103
Despair.	130
Devastated.	17
Did You Ever?.	135
Did You See Past Your Nothing?.	95
Do This.	89
Doubtless.	142
Down on Your Knees.	65
Dreams Hanging in the Air.	16
Dying Young.	129
Electric Air.	46
Et Tu.	76
Even, Even If It's Just A Fling.	22
Every Day Enchanting.	126
Fairytales.	48
Fame.	128
Fast.	117
Faust.	88
Feelin' Belief.	40
Fireflies.	14

Flatter, Flatter, Fall.	121
Fleeting.	152
For Lying Eyes.	24
Games.	52
Guessing Wrong.	134
He.	127
He Can't See Past.	97
Hey, Listen.	69
His Choice.	41
Hitchhikin'.	91
How Can You Not?.	147
How, When Will It Get Me?.	125
Hush.	117
Hymn of Religion.	131
I Can Hear It.	45
I Got S'More.	43
I Had a Heart Too:.	111
I Have an Obligation.	78
I Wish You Would Love Me.	145
I Woke Up.	96
I Won't Do It Anymore.	92
In Lebanon.	150
In the Blink of an Eye.	86
It Burns.	35
It's Okay.	94
It's the End Now.	74
It's Your Call.	75
Kiss Me, Sunshine.	106
Leaning Against the Wall.	37
Less Me.	132
Let's Split.	114
Like Religion.	12
Lit.	77
Live Like Light.	66
Love at Armageddon.	143
Love Dances.	76
Love is a Comedy.	32
Mem'ries.	137
Mi Amor.	72
Misdirected Wrong.	27
My Covers.	101
My Roses and My Wine.	149

No Tatters.	82
Not a Prize.	120
Not Bored.	28
Nothing Less.	30
Ocean Shore.	71
On Heaven or Earth.	26
One Soul Lost.	84
Optimism..	151
Other Vision.	73
Oxygen.	24
Pointless.	81
Ready, Set, Crash.	91
Reputation..	139
Risk Inverted.	13
Rue.	44
Seas and Deserts Part Us.	58
See Me There.	18
Seeing in the Dark..	83
Seer.	109
Send Heaven.	15
Sentinel.	104
Settling.	145
Silent Pianos.	7
Sitting With God..	34
Smoldered Ice.	116
So I Wait.	149
Somewhere Out There.	87
Spark and Crackle.	28
Sparked.	33
Spike It Up.	115
Spirits.	19
That Look.	27
The Belly..	130
The Dark.	63
The Dissident.	113
The Matter of Things.	9
The Subway.	140
The Unexpected Arrow..	110
This Broken Light.	62
This Exquisite Need.	66
This Moment in Time.	123
This Off-Course Bird.	61

Throw Away.	68
To Be Mended.	38
To Touch God's Face.	108
Treasured Now.	68
Turn My Light On.	105
Unrequited Questions.	14
Untiring.	55
Used Too.	42
VHS Control.	36
Waiting in Crystals.	51
Wake Up Love.	53
Wants.	21
Watchin'.	116
Watching Them Walk.	118
Well What Do You Know?.	122
What You Wait For.	99
What's Me?.	37
What's to Happen.	103
When We Are Old.	80
Words.	56
You and I.	141
You Are Realness.	11
You Don't.	58

About the Author

Rhonda J. Dolen

Rhonda Jennifer Dolen was born in 1980 in East Texas. From age four until age 21 she lived in California's Central Valley.

She attended California State University, Stanislaus where she received a B.A. in history. She moved to Arkansas in 2003 and attended graduate school at the University of Arkansas, Fayetteville where she received a M.A. in political science. During the graduate program, she concentrated on comparative politics and international relations and taught American National Government.

After graduate school, she attended law school for a year and a half, but decided that it was not for her. At the second law school she attended, she was first in her class of 19 for the semester of her attendance.

She wrote most of the poetry in this book during her twenties. The poems are fictional. When writing poems, she thinks of an image or idea and tries to convey it to the reader. The poems come to her quickly. She writes most poems in only a few minutes. When she is inspired, they flow almost completely intact from her mind to her pen, one line after the other.

She currently resides in central Pennsylvania. She likes to write about love and politics. She enjoys spending her free time visiting the beach with friends and family or wandering around New York City. She also likes action movies and cooking healthy food or rich desserts. Her favorite drink is Framboise, a sweet raspberry beer.

www.ingramcontent.com/pod-product-compliance
Lightning Source LLC
Chambersburg PA
CBHW071458080526
44587CB00014B/2142